THE
POWER *of*
PREACHING

THE KINGDOM PASTOR'S LIBRARY

THE
POWER *of*
PREACHING

CRAFTING A CREATIVE EXPOSITORY SERMON

TONY EVANS

MOODY PUBLISHERS
CHICAGO

Scripture quotations marked NASB are taken from the New American Standard Bible®, Copyright © 1960, 1962, 1963, 1968, 1971, 1972, 1973, 1975, 1977, 1995 by The Lockman Foundation. Used by permission. (www.Lockman.org)

Edited by Kevin P. Emmert and Michelle Sincock
Interior design: Erik M. Peterson
Cover design: Thinkpen Design
Cover photo of pulpit copyright © 2018 by Pearl/Lightstock (31332). All rights reserved.

All websites and phone numbers listed herein are accurate at the time of publication but may change in the future or cease to exist. The listing of website references and resources does not imply publisher endorsement of the site's entire contents. Groups and organizations are listed for informational purposes, and listing does not imply publisher endorsement of their activities.

ISBN: 978-0-8024-1830-2

We hope you enjoy this book from Moody Publishers. Our goal is to provide high-quality, thought-provoking books and products that connect truth to your real needs and challenges. For more information on other books and products written and produced from a biblical perspective, go to www.moodypublishers.com or write to:

Moody Publishers
820 N. LaSalle Boulevard
Chicago, IL 60610

1 3 5 7 9 10 8 6 4 2

Printed in the United States of America

*[Paul was] preaching the kingdom of God and
teaching concerning the Lord Jesus Christ
with all openness, unhindered.*

ACTS 28:31

*For Ezra had set his heart
to study the law of the LORD and to practice it,
and to teach His statutes and ordinances in Israel.*

EZRA 7:10

CONTENTS

INTRODUCTION

———————— ◆ ————————

The pastor who is serious about the Word of God and biblical, expositional preaching has a twofold challenge. He must not only bring the Word to people, but also bring people to the Word. In days gone by, when there was a consistent Judeo-Christian worldview that enveloped Western culture, people readily listened to God's Word. Even if they weren't going to act on God's Word, they had enough respect for it to go to church. They wanted to hear what the Bible had to say. But as our culture has become more and more secularized, as postmodernism has become the order of the day, people don't hear the Word as readily and naturally as they used to. So we must now bring people to the Word because they are not as aware of their need for the Word of God. Secularism and postmodernism have removed absolute truth from our understanding of reality. To many people, Scripture is no longer the standard by which reality is measured, and the concept of God has become just that—a concept. He's not a living, breathing being who wants us to hear and obey what He has to say. Many are abandoning the church and the pulpit because, unfortunately, they do not see the relevancy of God's Word in our contemporary society.

Even though we are living in an age of rebellion against authority, we're also living in an age where people are passionate for answers. They're going to social media in droves. They're looking in errant locations for solutions to their depression, anxiety, frustrations, chaos, divisions, and divorce. Does God have answers, and does He have it in language that today's person can understand and relate to? It's our job and opportunity as preachers to guide people to answers in God's Word, to draw people back to God for answers that they desperately need—in their lives, in their families, in the church, and in society at large.

So the preacher must be both attuned to the world in which he lives and faithful to God's Word so that people are drawn to the reality of God and to the answers that God's Word gives through his preaching. The Bible was written with relevance for today, and it must be preached powerfully in a relevant manner so that people see that the Word of God is not extinct. It is real and right, potent and pulsating with power. And that power should be seen when the preacher stands up and his conviction comes through. He believes what the Word says, and he can validate it through the exposition of Scripture. People need a kingdom pastor, manning a kingdom pulpit, with a kingdom proclamation, from God's kingdom book—the powerful Word of God.

CHAPTER ONE

FOUNDATION

◆

The call to preach is manifested in a burning desire to communicate God's truth. It resonates within as a passion that cannot be shaken nor removed. The Holy Spirit Himself sets people apart for the distinct role of preaching (Acts 13:2). The call to preaching is a personal invitation by God that you cannot run from. If God has called you to preach, He will chase you down until you accept His call.

One of the great identifiers of preachers who are "called," as opposed to those who do it to fulfill a job description, is found in the answer to a simple question: If you could do anything else, would you? When the answer to that question is "yes," then the answer of "calling" has also been revealed as "no." A preacher proclaims God's truth because He is compelled to (see Jer. 20:9; 1 Cor. 9:16). Now, whether he carries out his calling well depends largely on his investment in his own spiritual life, spiritual disciplines, study, preparation, and congregational relationships. These are things that this book, and other similar books, seek to strengthen in men called to preach. But the calling itself comes from God Himself and must serve as the foundation upon which all these tools and materials are laid.

Thus, how can you as a pastor personally know that you are called to preach before you head any more deeply into the content in this book? It's simple. If you are called by God to preach, He will give you an insatiable passion to preach. In addition to other ministry burdens that pastors have, high on that list must be the burden to proclaim God's truth. Pastor, do you have an insatiable passion to preach? By "insatiable" I mean that this passion will keep you up at night just thinking of passages you want to preach and biblical principles you hope to convey. You would preach for free if you had to (and yes, I know, many of you do!). Paul said, "woe is me" if I do not preach the gospel (1 Cor. 9:16). Jeremiah wrote in Scripture that he tried not to do it, but it became like fire shut up in his bones (Jer. 20:9). To be called by God to do something always comes with a passion you cannot shake.

Don't tell me you are called to preach and yet don't have a passion to do it. Because either you haven't been called, or you are so carnal that God can't get through to you. Whomever God calls, He emboldens. He creates the passion. This is why people who are called to preach keep talking about how they tried to run from it, but they couldn't get away. God tracked them down. Identify your calling first; then look at how the Bible itself describes a preacher to see how you fit into this summation or can adapt in order to better mirror it. Preaching involves so much more than standing up to speak. It is more than a task to do; it is to be an ongoing mindset. If you aren't willing to make it that, you may want to consider another profession because God says He will hold teachers to a higher level of accountability (James 3:1).

KINGDOM PREACHING

The greatest summary in Scripture of what a preacher is comes from a preacher named Solomon:

> In addition to being a wise man, the Preacher also taught the people knowledge; and he pondered, searched out and arranged many proverbs. The Preacher sought to find delightful words and to write words of truth correctly. The words of wise men are like goads, and masters of these collections are like well-driven nails; they are given by one Shepherd. (Eccl. 12:9–11)

This passage proclaims that a preacher must be given to personal reflection ("pondered"), study ("searched out"), and preparation ("arranged") so that he can preach in such a way that imparts spiritual knowledge. Masters at preaching maximize their messaging in such a way that their words goad their listeners toward Christ, our Shepherd. Any other result indicates that the mode of communication was a speech, not a sermon. Christ is the cornerstone and must be the centerpiece of our congregations' hearts and minds. While topics may differ and points of emphasis will vary, the overarching content of a sermon must always have the kingdom of God and the Lordship of our Shepherd and Savior, Jesus Christ, in view.

Luke affirmed this primary proclamation role of the preacher when describing the apostle Paul at the conclusion of the book of Acts, where he wrote, "And he stayed two full years in his own rented quarters and was welcoming all who came to him, preaching the kingdom of God and teaching concerning the Lord Jesus Christ with all openness, unhindered" (28:30–31). Over and over in Scripture, we read about the preaching of the kingdom of God and gospel of Christ. Here are just a few examples:

Jesus was going through all the cities and villages, teaching in their synagogues and proclaiming the gospel of the kingdom, and healing every kind of disease and every kind of sickness. (Matt. 9:35)

"This gospel of the kingdom shall be preached in the whole world as a testimony to all the nations, and then the end will come." (Matt. 24:14)

Now after John had been taken into custody, Jesus came into Galilee, preaching the gospel of God. (Mark 1:14)

Soon afterwards, He began going around from one city and village to another, proclaiming and preaching the kingdom of God. (Luke 8:1)

And He sent them out to proclaim the kingdom of God and to perform healing. (Luke 9:2)

"And heal those in it who are sick, and say to them, 'The kingdom of God has come near to you.'" (Luke 10:9)

The Law and the Prophets were proclaimed until John; since that time the gospel of the kingdom of God has been preached. (Luke 16:16)

But when they believed Philip preaching the good news about the kingdom of God and the name of Jesus Christ, they were being baptized, men and women alike. (Acts 8:12)

And he entered the synagogue and continued speaking out boldly for three months, reasoning and persuading them about the kingdom of God. (Acts 19:8)

When they had set a day for Paul, they came to him at his lodging in large numbers; and he was explaining to them by solemnly testifying about the kingdom of God and trying to persuade them concerning Jesus, from both the Law of Moses and from the Prophets, from morning until evening. (Acts 28:23)

Preaching must promote the kingdom of God and the name of Jesus Christ through the proclamation and application of the Word of God. In this way, the Holy Spirit transforms lives as people learn to live all of life under God's rule. Preaching is a partnership with the Spirit of God to draw listeners heavenward so that their lives are aligned with Christ's overarching rule. This can be accomplished only when the truth of His Word remains supreme and unpolluted. The Bible is the Word of God made up of the words of God. Thus, one of your primary responsibilities as a preacher is to be certain not to sprinkle human invention into His Word. Rather, you are there first and foremost to explain what God has already said.

In fact, God condemns the prophets for giving their own viewpoint or for tweaking what He has said. In Jeremiah 23:25–28, for example, we read,

> "I have heard what the prophets have said who prophesy falsely in My name, saying, 'I had a dream, I

had a dream!' How long? Is there anything in the hearts of the prophets who prophesy falsehood, even these prophets of the deception of their own heart, who intend to make My people forget My name by their dreams which they relate to one another, just as their fathers forgot My name because of Baal? The prophet who has a dream may relate his dream, but let him who has My word speak My word in truth. What does straw have in common with grain?" declares the LORD.

In today's language, we might interpret that last verse to say, "What does that which you are preaching have to do with the price of tomatoes?" If your words and thoughts counter God's Word and thoughts, then your words and thoughts are wrong and should not be shared from the pulpit. God makes that crystal clear, not only in Jeremiah, but elsewhere in Scripture as well. God will not bless, prosper, or anoint preaching that is not rooted in and resting on His truth. And, pastor, nothing could be worse than God being against your sermons.

EXPOSITORY PREACHING

A biblical expositor can be defined as *a spiritually prepared person declaring the interpretation and application of biblical truths acquired through the study of a passage in its context that the Holy Spirit then uses to confront the hearer and bring those who respond in conformity with God's Word.* Let's break up this definition and look at its parts. I'll begin by going over a few standard terms and definitions.

Hermeneutics: the science (principles) and art (task) by which the meaning of the biblical text is determined.

Exegesis: the determination of the meaning of the biblical text in its historical and literary contexts.

Exposition: the communication of the meaning of the text along with its relevance to present-day hearers.

Homiletics: the science (principles) and art (task) by which the meaning and relevance of the biblical text are communicated in a preaching situation.

Pedagogy: the science (principles) and art (task) by which the meaning and relevance of the biblical text are communicated in a teaching situation.

A Spiritually Prepared Person

When Jesus was confronted by Satan in the wilderness, He went to the Word. He demonstrated for us what we are to do for others as preachers. He reached back into the Old Testament, into a similar context, in order to apply what was said there to what He was facing in the present.

The passage in Deuteronomy 8 that He pulled from had to do with the Israelites wandering in the wilderness. The same problem of hunger and weakness plagued them then that battled Jesus in His present state. When they were hungry, God provided manna so they could have all that they needed to survive. By applying this passage to His own circumstance, Jesus essentially let the devil know that He didn't need his help because the same God who met Israel in the wilderness and came up with a feeding program from above was the same God He was looking to in His own situation of hunger. Why? Because God is the same yesterday, today, and forever, and how He handled things in the past remains relevant to us today.

Pastor, this is what an expositor does. He takes Scripture and shows us its relevancy for today. And the reason we must refer back to Scripture like Jesus did, rather than rely on our own thoughts, is because God's thoughts are not our thoughts. His ways are not our ways. As high as the heavens are above the earth, that's the difference between what we think and what God thinks (Isa. 55:8–9).

As you refine your craft as an expository preacher, you will also gain confidence that you never had before. You will preach with a new level of authority. It will give you a unified presentation because all of the parts will now relate to your point, which will be rooted and embedded in Scripture. Biblical exposition will also help you identify pitfalls because as you seek to relate everything back to the basic, biblical point, you will see areas where you need to go deeper in your study because you don't fully understand it yet or can't fully make the connection.

Expository preaching changes you, not just your hearers. Being bound to the order and content of the biblical text also means that expository preaching will change how you approach sermon preparation and preaching. Ezra 7:10 is one of the fundamental descriptions of who a preacher is. Memorize this verse. Let it be your definition as a preacher. It says, "For Ezra had set his heart to study the law of the LORD and to practice it, and to teach His statutes and ordinances in Israel." Ezra said he not only wanted to know the Word, but he also wanted to live the Word. He wanted to be a prepared person.

Some preachers hate going into the study and preparing for a sermon. They would rather be with people. They despise outlines, understanding figurative language, and the like. Yet perhaps this is because they have a warped perspective on study. Many preachers preach for the benefit of the people.

Yet if you follow Ezra's lead (which I hope you do), you will discover that preaching is first and foremost for yourself. Instead of studying and preaching for someone else, study and preach for yourself while letting others in on what you learn. This changes why you go into the study. You are now not just going into your study time because your church or class needs a sermon or lesson. You are also going in to ask God to teach *you*. This gives you a different mindset. Like Ezra, you will study in order to first put what you've learned into practice. Then you will teach what you've learned. You will find when you approach your preaching from this perspective that your sermons begin to feel more authentic and genuine than before. They will resonate with your audience at a deeper heart-level than before. You will desire to live and proclaim biblical truth in such a way that the spiritual principle and application takes root in the hearer *and* in yourself, enabling the Holy Spirit to produce ongoing growth.

Admonishing Timothy in his responsibilities as a preacher and teacher at the church in Ephesus, Paul wrote, "Until I come, give attention to the *public* reading *of Scripture*, to exhortation and teaching" (1 Tim. 4:13; emphasis added). In other words, Paul wanted Timothy to read it, live it, and teach it. That is biblical exposition in a nutshell. Paul also wanted Timothy's own spiritual development, based on his time in God's Word, to be visibly evident to his congregation (see 4:14–15).

In 1 Timothy 4:16, Paul follows up with these words to his mentee: "Pay close attention to yourself and to your teaching; persevere in these things, for as you do this you will ensure salvation both for yourself and for those who hear you." Timothy and the people he is teaching are already saved. But Paul is not talking about *justification* in this passage; he is talking about *sanctification*. He is talking about how doing those things in verse 13 would ensure the spiritual development of himself and those who hear him.

The point is that a preacher must first preach for himself if he wants to ensure the spiritual development of those to whom he preaches. If and when he doesn't, he is sabotaging the spiritual growth of those he has been tasked with shepherding. Yet if and when he does, he will grow personally by leaps and bounds. His spiritual growth will be off the charts. As a result, those whom he disciples will also grow underneath his covering and care.

Declaring Biblical Truths

Next, biblical exposition is a proclamation of a biblical truth. To appreciate what I mean, you and I have to understand one fundamental truth: the Bible is literature. Scripture is Holy Spirit-inspired literature, but it is still literature. Words have meaning, but words only have meaning in a context. For example, if I said the word *bark*, some of you would think I meant what a dog does. Others might assume I was talking about a tree. In order to form an idea, you have to put words together in such a way that they complete the idea or concept. What you want in biblical exposition is not merely the understanding of words, but also the understanding of words in relationship to other words. In this way, you can derive the idea or concept of Scripture.

Now, I hate to give you some discouraging news, but when people leave your church or Sunday school class, they are going to forget over ninety percent of everything you told them. You may come back to them in a few days and find they don't remember a single thing you said. Even if you taught in a tight, five-point outline, it is unlikely that they could rattle off even two of those carefully crafted points.

However, what they will remember is the overall idea. They are going to remember the concept. And they will also remember the application, if you made it clearly. This is why every time you preach a sermon or deliver a lesson, you must emphasize and re-emphasize the point. Have you ever talked to someone who rambles? If you're like me, you may want to interject a question: "What is your point?" You want them to identify a point because you need something in the communication process to attach to. Thus, there ought to be a succinct summary of your sermon or lesson so a hearer can remember the point, even when they forget everything else you said.

That said, I will generally have one major point per sermon and then come at that point in a variety of ways.

Whether that is through stories, biblical texts, or illustrations, I will keep coming back to this major point because I have learned in over fifty years of preaching that people simply can't remember everything you say. You have to leave them with something to grasp.

And if my goal in preaching is to make a lasting point that will move people closer to God, I can do this only if they can remember the point I made. Pastor, that's your job too. You want to make the point, emphasize and explain the point, and then apply the point so that everybody gets the point.

Biblical exposition is essential for any preacher because you have been called to clearly communicate God's words. Similar to the Ethiopian eunuch who asked for assistance in understanding what the passage in Isaiah meant (Acts 8:26–40), we all need guidance and spiritual insight to understand what God has said and what He means. A person can read the Bible without grasping the truths contained within it. In fact, pastors can do the same. Thus, biblical exposition is necessary so that clarity can be both gained and given.

Without an understanding and application of Scripture, Christians are left illiterate in regard to functioning as disciples of Christ. If we as pastors desire our congregants to live for the kingdom of God, we must equip them to understand and apply the Word of God. The Bible has real-life answers to real-life questions. And people need to know what those answers are. But if that person does not know how to approach

God's Word, or if the sermons they hear preached do not guide them to the Word, then the pastor has failed in his role. A pastor always ought to drive his congregation back to the text in order for the Holy Spirit to speak clearly through the Word.

When expository preaching is done right, congregants are encouraged to interact not only with you as the preacher, but also the Bible itself. Expository preaching compels listeners to search their Bibles as you preach, and it drives them to the Scripture throughout the week as they ponder the points you made and the questions you raised. Pastor, if people come to your church every week but never read their Bibles, something is wrong.

I have never enjoyed vegetables. Yet I was raised in a home where vegetables were a regular part of every meal. When squash was offered, I would try to pass it by. Regardless of my attempts, though, my mother would remind me whose house I was in: her house. So I had to abide by her rules, meaning I would have to eat my squash. She knew I needed my vegetables, despite my distaste for them. In fact, she usually said, "Tony, it's good for you," as she scooped a larger-than-necessary portion onto my plate.

What do vegetables have to do with preaching? Sometimes your congregation doesn't know what is good for them. They don't know how critical spiritual and biblical principles are for their everyday lives. They may view the Bible as an outdated, over-sized, boring book and spend their time engaging something else rather than searching the Scriptures. But as the pastor, you need to serve the Word in such a way that they come face to face with the truths of Scripture. As you do, they may develop a hunger for it on their own.

Paul warns Timothy of this bent in humanity toward a disregard for biblical truth. In 2 Timothy 4:3, he writes, "For the time will come when they will not endure sound doctrine; but wanting to have their ears tickled, they will accumulate for themselves teachers in accordance to their own desires." Pastor, that time has come; that time is now. People gravitate toward teaching that will scratch their itch rather than strengthen their souls. But when difficulties arise in life, an "itched ear" won't provide any help at all.

As a preacher, your role involves more than motivation and inspiration—though those are critical. You have the opportunity and responsibility to teach your congregation how to study and glean wisdom from Scripture. You do this through expository preaching, which forces learners to the Scripture. It encouragers hearers to understand how you got to a certain conclusion, which then helps them to use their own Bible as a source for uncovering truths on their own.

Another important reason why biblical exposition is critical is that the Holy Spirit speaks through the Word. The Holy Spirit is called "the Spirit of truth" (John 16:13). In fact, if the Word is not strong and clear when you preach it, then it is because you have not given the Holy Spirit anything to use. Often, sermons fall on deaf ears simply because the Spirit of God was not part of the process in either preparation or proclamation. You can preach words from the Bible without having spiritually empowered sermons. This is possible, unfortunately, when the Holy Spirit has not been made an integral part of the process (see 1 Cor. 2:4).

Study in Context

The final reason I want to share why biblical exposition is so critical is the need to return people to biblical theology. By "biblical theology" I am referring to something different from "systematic theology." Systematic theology is when you pull from various parts of the Bible in order to come up with a summary or a conclusion of what you want to teach. Systematic theology is a valuable approach to Scripture. However, this is not how the Bible was written. The Bible was written over a period of 1,600 years by 40 different authors from various walks of life. It was compiled to address specific problems that people faced at that time. Context, culture, and intention are critical aspects within each verse, chapter, and book. So biblical theology asks questions such as:

"What did the author intend to convey when he wrote to these people about this issue?"

"When this passage was written, what were the particular aspects of the culture?"

"Who is the intended audience?"

"What is the history and personality of the writer?"

Some passages of Scripture are difficult to grasp only because pastors and congregants are looking through the lens of systematic theology rather than biblical theology. In other words, they begin with what the Bible says as a whole rather than starting with what the author of that passage is teaching the audience of that time. Biblical theology forces people to examine the context.

Now, don't misunderstand me. I'm not saying that systematic theology is unimportant or unnecessary. It is. Systematic theology creates boundaries within which biblical theology can reside, much like the boundary lines and rules in a football game. But biblical theology provides the specific plays, direction, and player movements within those boundaries.

Biblical theology goes a step further in forcing you to understand what that text itself means in context. John, the disciple whom "Jesus loved," approached his compilation of Christ's teachings differently from the former tax-collector and kingdom-minded disciple we know as Matthew. Context allows for variations of personality, culture, audience, and more—which then gives greater insight and a more accurate understanding of the intended meaning of a passage as well as the spiritual principles for personal application.

Now, let me say a word about common misconceptions of biblical exposition. First, it is not exegetical preaching, as some assume. Exegetical preaching entails telling people what a certain Greek word is and where the word came from, or what the Hebrew cognate is. This type of preaching goes into great detail and provides a lot of information that most people may not know what to do with.

For example, if I come to your house for dinner, I don't need to know how you cooked the meal or every ingredient you used. All I need to know is that it has been well-prepared. Similarly, when people come to church, they don't need to know every step you took to prepare your sermon. They just want to know that it was well-prepared. That doesn't mean it is wrong to bring in a little insight here or there. Specific explanations may help your congregation understand the depth or meaning of a particular word or phrase. But the purpose of doing so is to deal with the word's or phrase's meaning and relevance, not just to show how much you know or how hard you worked. Too many pastors like to toss a Hebrew word or Greek phrase in somewhere just to demonstrate their own level of expertise. But that should not be the purpose for doing so or you will lose the interest of your congregation rather than gain it.

Second, just because a sermon was derived from the Bible doesn't make it expository. Some preachers like to preach verse by verse like a running commentary without looking for how those verses apply to their listeners. I have no issues against preaching verse by verse through a book; I've done it many times for our church on a large number of biblical books. But when you are preaching that way, you need to pay extra attention to application. In your preparation, you need to prayerfully seek out biblical application for your listeners.

Third, biblical exposition involves more than simply explaining the meaning of a passage in its historical context. In other words, telling people what Paul meant when he wrote something is only half of the equation. In order to truly preach expositionally, you must also make the transfer from what Paul told his audience at that time to what the Holy Spirit is seeking to teach you and your congregation in your time. If you don't make that transfer as a preacher, you have not completed the expositional process.

Confront the Hearer to Conform to God's Word

Biblical preaching confronts hearers *through* God's Word. It does not merely confront hearers *with* God's Word. Notice the difference. As a pastor, you don't just want people to know the Word. Your aim is for them to know God. When you go to a restaurant, you are handed a menu. To study the menu and not eat is a wasted trip because the purpose of the menu is to get the meal. To be able to say that you studied the menu is not enough. Restaurants exist to provide food, not just knowledge about food.

The goal of biblical exposition is to usher your listeners into a greater and deeper relationship with God Himself through the Word. It is not merely for them to become acquainted with God's Word.

You are part of the process God uses to confront your hearers. Don't deny or negate that. Many times in days gone by, pastors prayed something like, "Lord, hide me behind the cross as I proclaim your Word." But God doesn't want you hidden. He wants your personality to come through. He made you the way He wants you so that your gifts, nuances, and passions can strengthen, not diminish, the speaking and preaching of His Word. When you read Scripture, you will notice that Peter writes differently from the way Paul does. Paul writes differently from how James writes. You will always know a Pauline letter by his didactic style and very logical argumentation, while James gets up in your face and talks about all of your business, leaving all as fair game. On the other hand, John is the relational writer. He writes about what he does best: abiding. God didn't hide any of the authors' personalities. Rather, He used them.

That is why you must be *you*. Don't try to be Billy Graham.

If God wanted two Billy Grahams, He would have made two Billy Grahams. God needs one. And He needs one of you too. He wants you to express yourself as you prepare and preach, and He will use you and your uniqueness to confront others through the preaching of the Word.

When a church has stained glass windows, the light will come in through the glass and will reflect the variety of colors that make up the image. This is because the light that is colorless in and of itself comes through a prism of sorts to reflect a distinct hue. Two men may proclaim the same passage, yet because their personalities are different, it will be proclaimed with different colorations. God does not want us hidden as robots behind a pulpit. He designed us so that our distinctiveness and uniquenesses will show through.

God wants what He said to be understood and responded to. As a pastor, you can use your life experiences, lessons, personality, interests, and thought process to prepare and preach in a way that allows people to understand and respond to God's Word. Maximize all that God has given to you in order to explain the Word so that your congregants experience new life in Christ. Second Peter 1:2–4 states it clearly:

> Grace and peace be multiplied to you in the knowledge of God and of Jesus our Lord; seeing that His divine power has granted to us everything pertaining to life and godliness, through the true knowledge of

Him who called us by His own glory and excellence. For by these He has granted to us His precious and magnificent promises, so that by them you may become partakers of the divine nature, having escaped the corruption that is in the world by lust.

Pastor, you are not preaching just to grow a church. You are not preaching to increase the size of your personal platform. You are not preaching for applause. You are not even preaching to pay the bills. You are preaching to lead people to worship God and align their thoughts and actions to Him— life transformation. Knowledge alone will not produce life transformation; rather, the God of that knowledge will.

For example, the magi in the East learned of the star that would indicate the birth of Jesus. This led them on a tour that brought them face to face with the Son of the living God. Yet in the same passage of the Magi's worship experience, we also read about biblical scholars who also knew where to worship Jesus, but they never went there themselves.

We read in 2 Peter 1 that God designed His Word to serve as our personal "stars," leading us to worship and align our lives under God. It says in verses 19–21,

So we have the prophetic word made more sure, to which you do well to pay attention as to a lamp shining in a dark place, until the day dawns and the morning star arises in your hearts. But know this first of all, that no prophecy of Scripture is a matter of one's own interpretation, for no prophecy was ever made by an act of human will, but men moved by the Holy Spirit spoke from God.

Your goal as a pastor is to preach God's Word in such a way that those who hear you grow spiritually as they encounter God. Paul says in 1 Corinthians 9:19, "For though I am free from all men, I have made myself a slave to all, so that I may win more." Win more people to what? To Jesus Christ. A biblical preacher acts on God's behalf. When you preach, you stand as God's representative in the pulpit for Him to use to impart His truth to His followers. Just as Jesus walked on earth in everyday clothes and in an everyday posture to explain the supernatural God to everyday people (see John 1:18; 20:21), our job as preachers is to do something similar. You are a declarer of God's Word, a continuation of the explanation of His truth as His spokesman.

TEACHING VERSUS PREACHING

Perhaps here would be a good place to distinguish between preaching and teaching. The Bible says that Jesus came both preaching and teaching. This was true of the apostle Paul's ministry as well. You hear some people say they are a teacher of the Word, while others say they are a preacher. The pastor is called to do both.

The difference between the two lies in the emphasis. Preaching emphasizes motivation, application, and response. *Preaching* is the word regularly used for evangelism in the book of Acts because preaching always had the aim of bringing a sinner to repentance or to a response to the gospel. It focuses on what the hearer is going to do with what they just heard. The prophets preached. To end their prophecy, they would always give a call to action. Biblical preaching seeks to persuade hearers to respond to the truth, not just inform them of the truth.

Teaching, though, focuses more on the details. Teachers emphasize understanding and want to ensure you get the information and know what the information means. A teacher is fundamentally concerned with clarifying the meaning of the subject. The teacher seeks to answer the questions of why, what, and how.

Now, every preacher has to do some teaching. However, every teacher in not necessarily a preacher. Keep that distinction in mind. One emphasizes motivation and response. The other emphasizes cognitive understanding. Expository preaching marries preaching and teaching together with the dual, overarching goal of advancing God's kingdom and exalting the lordship of Jesus Christ (see Acts 28:30, 31).

Yet whether you're preaching or teaching, you, as a

proclaimer of God's Word, stand between two worlds. You are a link between the world of the Bible and today's world of your audience. Your job is to take one hand and reach back to the Bible to understand and convey contextual, intentional meaning while taking your other hand and reaching out to your world to help your hearers understand and apply biblical principles in their lives.

In order to do this, two things need to happen. First, you must be a student of the Bible. Second, you must also be a student of contemporary culture. You must know how to exposit the Scripture while also knowing how to exposit the daily news feeds.

For example, I need to know not only what the Bible says about racial reconciliation, but also what the struggles are right now in our culture regarding race. Thus, the expository preacher merges these two worlds. It is a spiritual exercise to preach, declaring the interpretation and application of biblical truth.

CHAPTER TWO

ORGANIZATION

———————— ◆ ————————

Pastor, you have to take pains with preaching. You cannot just throw together a Saturday night special and expect to fulfill your role as a preacher. Preaching ought always to involve work and organization. That's why you need to be sure of the one thing we emphasized in the last chapter: that you are called to do what you are doing.

But just because you are called to preaching doesn't guarantee you will be successful at it. And by "successful," I am referring to helping bring about life transformation in those who hear you preach. What would happen if an NFL player decided not to practice or chose to keep a busy schedule filled with everything but football? We all know what would happen: that player would no longer play for the NFL. Similarly, a preacher must put in the work required to organize his life, time, thoughts, and words in such a way as to be fully prepared to deliver the sermon God has called him to deliver.

And you must couple your organization and preparation with a spirit of prayer. The act of prayer is not only part of your relationship with God, but also part of your work as a preacher. As the late missionary Hudson Taylor once said, "Prayer *is* the work." For far too many preachers, prayer is like the National Anthem before a football game. It gets the game started but has absolutely nothing to do with what is happening on the field. Rather, prayer should be compared to the football itself. Without it, there is no game at all. Prayer is critical to preaching because prayer engages the presence of the Holy Spirit. If you desire for the Word of God to impact your listeners, you must bathe your preparation and presentation in prayer.

Not only that, you have to be disciplined and set aside time for study. Second Timothy 2:15 says, "Be diligent to present yourself approved to God as a workman who does not need to be ashamed, accurately handling the word of truth." You have to work at accurately handling God's Word.

I set aside my Wednesdays for an ongoing and uninterrupted time in God's Word in which I study and prepare the foundation for my two sermons that week. I preach both on Wednesday night and Sunday morning. But I also get up early most days for consecrated time in God's Word, in His presence, because accurately handling God's truth doesn't come about by dipping in here or there.

Most preachers are designed, from a personality standpoint, for the delivery. We enjoy seeing the "lightbulb" moment in the eyes of our listeners or hearing an "amen" or applause, letting us know that their spirits and souls are being touched and transformed. But there is no applause in the study, just like there is no applause in the gym for an athlete. But if you don't approach the gym in a disciplined, consistent manner as an athlete, your career won't last long. Just like no NFL player would ever say that practice on Thursdays is enough for the game, no preacher should rely on a minimal amount of personal study, application, and abiding with God.

CREATING A PREACHING CALENDAR

Not only should you spend time in personal study and application while preparing for your message, but you also need to set aside time to create your preaching calendar. Don't let yourself wonder on Friday what you will preach on Sunday.

Some people create their preaching calendars while in the office. I go away for a weekend on two or three different occasions throughout the year. I then seek to lay out the foundation of my preaching calendar for the next three to six months. I lay out my series concept and the progression of that concept from one week to the next, and I choose the basic themes and passages. That way when I go into my study time each week, I already have a starting point as well as know the main idea I want to communicate. Knowing this prevents a crisis situation. However, I am not bound to this schedule. I can change it as events or circumstances demand, but at a minimum, it serves as a guide.

For example, this year, I chose to do an eight-week series on biblical manhood entitled: "Adam, Where You At?" This series hadn't been laid out in my preaching calendar. I had planned to just preach one sermon on the topic. But the congregational response was so warm, receptive, and needed—and the current climate of our culture is deprived of a lot of biblical teaching on manhood—that I chose to extend the single sermon seven more weeks into a full series. So while it is good to plan your preaching calendar, you also need to leave room for the Holy Spirit to guide you and to allow yourself the humility to listen to those who are listening to you.

In choosing your content calendar, keep in mind that sermons should include a mixture of elements, much like a well-balanced meal. When there is a healthy mixture in your sermon calendar, people leave nourished and satisfied. When I create my content calendar, a "balanced diet" entails preaching through one book of the Bible per year, one doctrine per year, and also one popular contemporary topic per year—such as marriage, spiritual warfare, or life purpose.

It's important to preach through books of the Bible because your congregants need to see authors and themes unfold and get to know larger sections of Scripture more fully. Plus, a book will typically cover a lot of different subjects. One way to approach preaching through books of the Bible in the Old Testament is to do personality studies. For example, if you plan to preach through Genesis, you realize that most of the Old Testament is narrative literature. They are stories. So you focus in on the stars of those stories. You could preach on Abraham, Jacob, Joseph, and more.

When you choose your series to cover a specific doctrine, you are discipling your congregation with regard to key, foundational beliefs they need. There are a myriad of Christian doctrines to preach through. If you don't know where to start, I recommend getting my book *Theology You Can Count On* or *Basic Theology* by Dr. Charles Ryrie. These one-volume books cover all the major doctrines as well as scriptures related to those doctrines (see Appendix A for more resources).

As far as choosing contemporary topics to preach through, keep your ears open to what comes up in pastoral counseling sessions. You must also address cultural issues people are facing, both socially and politically. Spend time working through these life issues because preaching involves discipling your members on how to handle life's scenarios from a biblical, kingdom worldview. (For more on the process of creating a master preaching calendar, see "Creating a Master Preaching Calendar.")

THE PROCESS OF STUDY

After you determine your topics in the preaching calendar, you then study the Scriptures. You begin to determine what each passage means. The easiest way to do this is through **observation**. This is where you take out a pen and a yellow pad (at least I do) or a computer, and simply start writing out everything you see in the passage. You are not to the point of analyzing what you see. If you start to integrate study into this portion, you will reduce the amount of things you observe. In observation, you are simply giving yourself the time and space to collect data. If there are certain observations you don't understand, put a check mark by them to indicate they need further study. Or if there are observations you know will be more important than others when you map out your message, circle or underline them so they will catch your attention when it's time to review your notes. In your observation process, always keep in mind that you need to observe what comes before and after the particular passage you are studying. This will help give you context on what you are studying.

Following observation comes **interpretation**. Because this part of sermon preparation is so critical, I've dedicated an entire chapter to it in this book. So I'll touch on it only briefly here. Interpretation is when you dig into the content using study tools such as commentaries, Bible dictionaries, and virtual study tools like Logos or Blue Letter Bible to give you insight into the meaning of the passage.

Following observation and interpretation, you want to **determine your main point**. To do this, ask yourself two questions:

> *What is the main subject of this passage?*
>
> *What is this passage saying about this subject?*

Once you have answered these two questions, you can use the answers to inform your decision on crafting your main point. Spend time considering what you hope to convey to your hearers from the passage. Also consider what the Lord is impressing upon you to focus on.

Next, **determine the purpose**. Ask yourself,

> *What do I want this sermon to accomplish in the minds, hearts, and lives of the listeners?*

Without a purpose, you will wander aimlessly because you will not have a focal point to which to direct your hearers.

After you solidify your main point and purpose, you then **outline your presentation**. This is how you want to progress through making your point and establishing your purpose. You want your sermon to develop intentionally. An outline is simply taking your points based on the passage and putting them into a logical flow so you know where you are going. If you don't know where you're going, then no one else will know either. Outlines establish an orderly movement of ideas so listeners will be able to track with you. The key is making sure all the points relate to one another and to the passage on which you are speaking. I like for each of the points to be a grammatically complete statement—not a question. I then incorporate the major idea wherever it most naturally occurs in the sermon. For clarity, I then put transitions in parentheses between the points. And I use Roman numerals for the main points—but not for my introduction or conclusion.

There are three kinds of outlines that a preacher can use. I recommend you familiarize yourself with all three and find the one that works best for you:

1. The *exegetical* outline states the concepts and structure of the text in terms of the original author and recipients. Such an outline tends to use technical language that conveys the semantic force of the textual assertions (for example: reason, manner, means, purpose, context, sphere, source—the statements).

2. The *expositional* outline states the exegetical outline in terms of its timeless and universal principles. Such an outline conveys the semantic force of the principles without the use of technical language.

3. The *homiletical* outline states the strategy for communicating the concept of the text to a specific, contemporary audience.

(You can find examples of each of these outlines in "Types of Outlines.")

Following the establishment of your point, purpose, and outline, you want to *apply the idea*. Provide a clear application for listeners to take with them. Be intentional about creating the application so it can relate to people in various walks of life. When you study, imagine a variety of people around you such as a stay-at-home mom, a career person, an athlete, and more. Let these invisible people ask you questions. Because when you begin to answer numerous questions from various people, you will make your content relevant to a greater number of hearers.

After your application, *determine your conclusion and introduction*. The purpose of the conclusion is to review the idea and drive it home. You want to use this part of the message to make it stick. As in any conclusion, revisit the main point of your message. But try not to use this time to revisit all the sub-points of your message. This is an opportunity to leave your hearers with a memorable illustration that touches on what you have been preaching about.

Determine your introduction last because until you have

your message mapped out, you won't know what you are introducing. The purpose of your introduction is twofold. First, it needs to orient your listeners to the idea you are about to present. Second, it needs to make them want to hear the idea. You want to capture their attention, and this can be done a variety of ways. Many preachers begin their sermons with a joke or two. You can also consider opening your sermon with a personal illustration. Whatever the case, try not to fall into a rut of beginning your sermons the same way every time.

To help you in your preparation, I'm including two checklists in the back of this book from a preaching course I taught at Dallas Theological Seminary for you to use in your personal preparation. One is called "Creating a Master Preaching Calendar" and the other is "Creating a Sermon." Use these as guides only, not rules. Let them help you establish your own approach that fits best with your personality, history, and interests while also remaining within the boundaries of solid biblical exposition.

CHAPTER THREE

PREPARATION

◆

Some years ago, I had the privilege of visiting both China and India. Being in each nation was an incredible experience as I got to see entirely different cultures and ways of life in action. But I had several handicaps in these countries because they were foreign territory to me.

My biggest challenge was the inability to speak the native languages. I also did not understand the various cultural practices and beliefs, so in some cases, I couldn't fully appreciate what I was seeing. I was limited culturally as well as linguistically, and I needed someone to help me maneuver my way through these lands that were new and strange to me.

When they meet someone who is obviously a visitor, Texans say, "You aren't from these parts, are you?" I most definitely was not from any "parts" of China or India, and my trips might have been disasters except for one factor: I had an interpreter to stand beside me and translate what I was hearing into a language I could understand and respond to.

If you have ever tried to communicate with someone in a language not your own, you know how difficult it can be. Even with an interpreter who knows both languages, there are always times when you are stymied, either because the interpreter is searching for the right word in the other language to accurately convey your English word, or vice versa. And interpretation is almost never just a matter of doing a straight word-for-word translation.

Now, you may think challenges arise only when going from one language to another. But some people who speak the same language and even live under the same roof still can't communicate well with each other. Even a shared language can be a huge barrier to communication when there is uncertainty about the meaning of our words.

I can illustrate this by mentioning the word *lead*. You have no way of knowing for sure which meaning I have in mind until I use it in a sentence. That's because these four simple letters can be a verb that means "to direct," a noun that means "a position in front," or an adjective that means "to act or serve as the lead," as in the lead story in a newspaper. These meanings are at least related in concept, but they don't exhaust the possibilities for confusion. The word *lead* has an entirely different meaning, and even a different pronunciation, when it refers to a soft metal. And even beyond this, we have the word *led* that sounds just like the name of that soft metal, but is the past tense of the verb *lead*.

So now, even if I told you I was thinking of the word *lead* and pronounced it with the short *e* instead of the long *e,* you still couldn't be absolutely certain what I meant until I used the word in a sentence that clarified its meaning. In other words, you are in the dark until I interpret the word in context and thus reveal its meaning to you so we can understand each other.

If one small and seemingly simple word like *lead* requires that much interpretation to make sense, think of all the possibilities for miscommunication and misunderstanding in the thousands of words in the English language—to say nothing of the thousands of other languages and dialects on earth. In the case of the Scripture, the message has to navigate through language barriers (since it was originally written in ancient languages we no longer speak) and the barriers of time and culture for us to interpret what the originator of the message meant.

Now let's take this one step further and think about how totally ill-equipped sinful human beings are to understand God's message from heaven without someone to interpret it. How could a perfectly holy God communicate with a sinful race on a tiny speck of His creation called earth? He did it in two ways: by becoming a man Himself in the person of His

Son and by giving us His written Word in human languages that were designed to be read and understood.

You may remember from your high school or college classes that communication involves three elements. There is an encoder, the person sending the message; a decoder, the person receiving the message; and the message itself. The goal of communication is to make sure that the data the decoder receives is what the encoder intended to send so the message doesn't get lost in transit.

We don't have to worry that the message got distorted during the transmission of the Bible from God's mouth to our hands. God Himself is the encoder in the person of the Holy Spirit, and the message is His Word sent to the "decoders," the human writers of Scripture. Our task is not to receive new revelation, but to understand the revelation God has given us. This task is interpretation, or the work of determining what the Holy Spirit meant by what He inspired the Bible's authors to record. Many people avoid the Bible because they say they can't understand it. When people say they can't understand the Bible, they are usually talking about the issue of interpretation. The technical word for this is *hermeneutics,* which comes straight from the Greek and is related to the god Hermes of Greek mythology, whose job was to communicate the language of the gods to human beings. Biblical hermeneutics is the science and art of interpreting the Bible.

Hermeneutics is a science because words have meanings that we can rely on, and languages follow certain rules of grammar and composition that can be observed and cataloged. But hermeneutics is also an art because just trying to match up words from one language to another is not enough to decipher what an author is saying.

When we talk about the meaning of a biblical text, we are after the original author's intent and not just what it says to us. Many pastors think that doing Bible study consists of figuring out what the Bible means to us. But that's not interpreting the Bible because one of the principles of good biblical interpretation is that a text has one primary meaning. It may have many personal applications, but the Bible does not mean whatever anyone wants it to mean. Most heresies begin with a twisted interpretation of the Scripture.

The exciting thing is that when you arrive at the right understanding of the Bible, along with the right application, there is no issue in life that cannot be addressed victoriously. Understanding and application join together to bring about transformation.

Yet this understanding and application has to come about through careful study. Studying Scripture in light of its original language is key to understanding the authors' intentions. The Old Testament was written almost entirely in the Hebrew language. (Small portions of the book of Daniel are written in Aramaic.) The New Testament was written in a common form of Greek we call *koinē* that is not spoken today. Jesus likely gave the Sermon on the Mount in Aramaic (it was the common language used in conversation in first-century Israel), yet it is recorded for us in Greek by the Gospel writers. Paul himself used Old Testament quotes taken from the Greek version of the Old Testament called the Septuagint (which was translated from the Hebrew beginning in the third century BC), and you and I are now more than likely using an English version of the Bible that translates these various languages so that we can read and understand God's Word.

All interpretation in some way begins with translation. Even a Bible translation in our own language may at times use words unfamiliar to us that require us to restate the word or phrase into a form that we better understand. This is just another form of translation, which means that the first tool in interpretation should always be a good, trustworthy, contemporary translation of Scripture. It is also good to have a few other translations on hand so that you can compare and contrast the choices that were made in translating particular words and phrases from the original languages. For my personal study, I primarily use the New American Standard Bible (NASB), but other solid, contemporary versions include the Christian Standard Bible (CSB), New International Version (NIV), the English Standard Version (ESV), the New Living Translation (NLT), and the New King James Version (NKJV).

Another area of deeper understanding shows up in the

gap that exists between history and culture. In the northern regions of the United States, some people refer to the rolling basket used to load groceries at the store as a buggy. In other regions this same basket is referred to as a cart. If an encoder (speaker) at a grocery store says to a decoder (listener), "Can I have a buggy?" and the decoder is not familiar with the term, then the message would require some discussion so that the term could be translated and understood.

Just imagine that one culturally and geographically embedded tradition of describing an object (in this case a basket for carrying food) spread across centuries of time and different world cultures. When you consider that grocery stores as we know them are a recent phenomenon (the first modern self-service grocery store—one that would require a buggy/cart—dates to 1916) and that prior to that you would shop at a general store or trading post for your dry, non-perishable goods and visit a butcher or local dairy for perishable foods, you can imagine how it can take some effort to understand even something as basic as how a particular culture during a particular time period stored, purchased, exchanged, and carried their food.

The latest date for a book of the Bible being written is likely in the 90s AD (the book of Revelation), which means that we are almost 2,000 years removed—historically and culturally—from the New Testament writers, and even further from the Old Testament writers. In addition, when you consider that the world of Scripture emerges from a Middle Eastern, rural, mainly agrarian culture, you can imagine the barriers this gap can present when we read the text of Scripture through our contemporary Western context.

In addition, the ancient history and cultures of the Bible can present traditions or practices that require some translation and interpretation to get at the intended meaning within Scripture. Studying and analyzing cultural norms, contexts, and language-based nuances during the time of the biblical writings help to provide insight into understanding the meaning of the text.

The Bible is meant to be an open book to anyone who wants to know the truth. But this does not mean that God simply throws His treasure chest of truth open to anyone who comes along so the person can look it over and take whatever he wants. Jesus called that "throw[ing] your pearls before swine" (Matt. 7:6). Studying Scripture requires diligent work. It also requires certain prerequisites to be present in our lives before the Bible becomes an open book to us.

THE WORK OF THE SPIRIT

The first prerequisite to understanding the Bible is intimate communion with God through the Holy Spirit. The closer you are with the Spirit, the more clearly you will understand the Word. This follows because the Holy Spirit is "the Spirit of truth" (John 16:13) whom God sent to continue the teaching that Jesus began while He was on earth.

The Holy Spirit's job is to interpret and clarify the truth—to reveal to you what it means and how you need to apply it to your life. But the Spirit does not do His work of teaching in a heart and mind that are closed to Him. I am referring to a believer who is out of sync with the Spirit for whatever reason, be it apathy or sin. Since the Holy Spirit is the illuminator and the interpreter of Scripture, it makes sense that the closer you are with Him, the clearer the Bible will become to you (see John 16:13).

Philip was guided by the Spirit as he explained the Scriptures to the Ethiopian eunuch in Acts 8. The Bible also says that when Peter had finished his sermon on the Day of Pentecost, the people "were pierced to the heart" (Acts 2:37) and cried out for help in knowing what to do next. The Holy Spirit is behind your job as a pastor in teaching God's people to understand His Word.

A second prerequisite to understanding the Bible has to do with our willingness to respond in obedience to what the Spirit shows us (see Ps. 119:34). Peter wrote, "Therefore, putting aside all malice and all deceit and hypocrisy and envy and all slander, like newborn babies, long for the pure milk of the word, so that by it you may grow in respect to salvation" (1 Peter 2:1–2). God wants us to rid ourselves of any sinful attitude that prevents us from growing as we feed on His

Word. Jesus promises to only disclose His truth to those who are prepared to obey it (John 7:17).

BASIC INTERPRETIVE METHODS AND TOOLS

Learning the Bible takes work. That's why Paul told Timothy, "Be diligent to present yourself approved to God as a workman who does not need to be ashamed, accurately handling the word of truth" (2 Tim. 2:15). The purpose of biblical exposition is comprehensive. Remember, a biblical expositor is *a spiritually prepared person who declares the interpretation and application of biblical truths acquired through contextual study of a passage that the Holy Spirit then uses to confront the hearer and bring those who respond in conformity with God's Word.*

Thus, preparation is key. The first step as you read the Bible is to ask some very basic interpretive questions about the passage you are reading. For instance, what does the text say? Try paraphrasing it back to yourself or summarizing what the passage says. Then you might ask to whom this passage was written and under what circumstances. Knowing a passage's original recipients and context can help unlock its meaning. Other basic interpretive questions to ask of any Bible passage include these: Is there a command here to be obeyed, a sin to avoid, a promise to claim, or a warning to heed? These are just some of the questions you can use to understand the Word.

You should also have some basic Bible study tools such as a concordance that lists every word in the Bible, a Bible commentary, and a Bible dictionary. A concordance enables you to cross-reference passages and quickly locate biblical references for topics and passages. It also allows you to examine how words were used in other places. For example, when Peter rebelled against God by denying Jesus Christ three times, Jesus later met him on the seashore. This is recorded for us toward the end of the book of John. We read in this passage that Peter jumped into the water and swam back to shore where Jesus was cooking breakfast over a charcoal fire. Now, if you were to use your concordance to look up the word "charcoal," you would discover that this particular word is used in only one other place in the entire Bible. What's more is that this one other place is when Peter denied Jesus while warming his hands over a charcoal fire. The very thing over which Peter warmed his hands when he denied Christ was identical to what Jesus cooked his meal over when He restored him. Jesus took him back to the place of his denial, confronted it symbolically, and then repositioned him for service. Using a concordance in your study enables you to identify patterns and symbols in Scripture that you likely wouldn't be able to otherwise.

In addition to a concordance, you need to acquire and

use a chronological study Bible as well as a Bible dictionary and encyclopedia. By using these tools, you can go to any subject in Scripture and find a summary discussion on the Bible's teaching in that realm. These resources will save you time as you prepare your messages. A chronological study Bible allows you to read Scripture in the order that the events actually happened. A Bible dictionary combines word meanings and proper words for biblical terms to enable the reader to clearly understand words and terms in the context of the theological concepts of that particular passage.

Also, there is so much available online that there should be no excuse for not handling the Word of God correctly. There are even online platforms such as Blue Letter Bible that allow you to look up the original language of each word in Scripture and see the context and definition of those words, as well as where else they appear in the Word. All of that is available to you for free. If you desire more access to in-depth study, you can look at paid platforms such as Logos, which comes complete with a plethora of commentaries, articles, linguistic tools, and more.

THE IMPORTANCE OF MEANING

The central task of hermeneutics is to look closely enough at the text that you understand its meaning and then carry the meaning across the time and culture bridge to your own setting. You can think of that bridge spanning the gap between the text and our own setting as being comprised of three sections or three steps: (1) *observation* (What does the text say?), (2) *interpretation* (What does the text mean?) and (3) *application* (How does the meaning of the text apply to my own time, and how should I respond in obedience?). This hermeneutical bridge is sometimes abbreviated as the OIA method.

To *observe* a passage of Scripture is to read the text closely enough that you can understand what the author was saying. One of the primary barriers to close observation is our own often-short attention spans. In these days of the internet and social media, we are used to reading quickly and distractedly, clicking through to new links, or checking the latest updates and new notifications that come our way. As a result, it becomes difficult for us to give sustained attention to anything we are reading, particularly when it might engage unfamiliar ideas, characters, or contexts like those of the ancient world. This means that to look closely and listen attentively to God's voice, we will need to retrain ourselves in the discipline of observation.

This discipline of observation, like any good habit, can be learned only through regular practice. A key tool to help in the discipline of observation is to refresh your command of the English language by understanding the basic rules of grammar. The word *grammar* is from a Greek word that means the art or technology of letters. It is the basic, under-lying rules for how authors communicate through writing. Understanding these rules helps you get at the point the author is making in an organized way.

Another important tool in this discipline of observation is asking good, penetrating questions about the text you are reading. I mentioned some earlier in this chapter as examples. The right question will help you to discern what the text is saying, and the right question can open up new insight into what God is saying to you through His Word. Another bene-fit of asking questions of the text is that the process slows us down. We need an intentional practice that will prevent us from missing things, one that will force us to see the partic-ular details the author is communicating. While not every single question will apply to each text, we should ask these five basic investigative questions when we approach a text:

1. *Who?* That is, who are the main characters in the text, who is the author, and to whom is the content written?

2. *What?* What is the action being described or the conversation happening?

3. *When?* When was the text written, or when did the activity take place?

4. *Where?* Where did the event or conversation take place, and where was the original audience located?

5. *Why?* Why are the actions and conversations presented and/or connected?

Through close observation, we come to grasp the particulars of the passage and discern what the author is saying. Yet in doing the work of observation, we often open the door to further questions. We understand the details of the passage, but we begin to wonder, why did the author arrange the details in this way? What was he trying to communicate to the audience? Such questions lead us to the next step on the OIA bridge: *interpretation*, the process of discerning what the selected text means.

This question of meaning is always anchored in understanding what the author intended to communicate to his audience. It is often helpful to write a paraphrase of the passage in your own words. Be exact in thought and take care to state the relationships of ideas, principles, and happenings you see within the text, whether the Bible states them explicitly or not. As you write, relate the parts of the passage to your main idea. Always change the statement of your main idea to fit the parts of a passage. Never bend the parts to fit your statement of the idea.

The text itself is not an independent reality that wills itself to mean something. The meaning of a text comes from the will of the author who intends a specific meaning in a specific context. So in discerning the meaning intended by the author, we must also interpret that meaning in light of God's intention to reveal Himself and His plan for His creation through the voice of these human authors of Scripture. Perhaps you have heard that the most important rule in real estate is "location, location, location." When it comes to this step of interpretation, the most important rule to understanding the meaning of the text is context, context, context. To understand what a text means, we need to consider the context of Scripture, the context of history and culture, and the context of Christ.

Have you ever experienced someone using a Bible verse as a "bumper sticker Scripture"—a verse or part of a verse pulled out of its context and made into a short, witty, motivational mantra that can fit on a car's bumper? You may have heard athletes quoting Paul's "I can do all things through [Christ] who strengthens me" (Phil. 4:13)—disregarding Paul's point that Christ can strengthen him for his mission regardless of his financial status—in favor of claiming this as a promise that Christ can help them overcome their athletic opponents. When we isolate a verse and read it outside of its setting in the Bible's larger narrative, we may fixate on ideas that are not supported by God's full revelation of Himself and His desires for the world that He created. To read within the context of Scripture is to recognize the genres of biblical literature and to recognize the progressive, unfolding story of the Bible.

If I began to read instructions like, "Use 1 and ¼ cups of butter, 2 cups of sugar, 3 large eggs . . ." you would recognize that I am reading a recipe. If I began with the phrase, "Once upon a time . . ." you would recognize my text as a fairy tale. Both of these are examples of a genre of literature, and once you recognize a writing's genre, you intuitively have a set of general expectations for how the rest of the text should be read and understood. A genre is a literary category that has shared characteristics, form, and subject matter. The Bible, like any other type of literature, is written in literary genres that would have been familiar to the original audience. To get closer to the meaning intended by the author, one of the first questions you should ask is, "What genre of literature am I reading, and how does that genre typically communicate meaning?" Below you will find descriptions of the six key biblical genres.

1. *Narrative*. This form of literature tells a story. Since the Bible is the story of God's self-revelation to His creation, it should not surprise us that narrative is the most common genre found in the Bible (40 percent of the Old Testament is narrative). Three primary types of narrative appear in Scripture:

History. Biblical history is uniquely focused on the narrative of God's past interaction with His world.

It can include the history of people groups and the histories of individual people as they relate to God's work in this world. Examples include the books of Exodus and Joshua.

Law. Within the Old Testament, you will often find the record of laws given to legislate the covenant between God and His people, Israel. These laws order the religious, social, and political life of God's unholy, broken people so the holy God can maintain His covenant relationship with them. Exodus, Numbers, and Deuteronomy all have examples of legal literature, though they also have elements of history, but the book of Leviticus is the clearest example of this genre.

The Gospels. Matthew, Mark, Luke, and John are centered on the life of Jesus Christ, and each tells the story of Jesus from a different perspective. In particular, each of the Gospels gives primary attention to the passion narrative: the story of Jesus's arrest, trial, crucifixion, death, burial, and resurrection.[1]

2. *Prophetic Literature*. We typically expect prophetic literature to have predictions about events still to come, but

---

1. The book of Acts is a transitional narrative from the life of Jesus to the doctrines of Jesus communicated in the Epistles.

often these predictions are focused on events, people, and nations that are in the past for readers living in the twenty-first century. The prophet was God's representative and was commissioned to warn God's people of the soon-coming consequences they would face if they continued to break God's covenant with them. Prophetic literature typically contains characteristics such as call narratives (a record of the call of a particular prophet), pronouncements of God's judgment—paired with promises of consolation and restoration—and frequent use of symbolic and metaphorical language to describe prophetic events. Prophecy also gives us a glimpse into God's heart as He mourns over the sin of His people and the judgment they will face, mingled with a divine love that refuses to reject His sinful, broken, but treasured people. All this makes prophecy one of the most difficult genres to interpret, and we are wise to use helps such as Bible dictionaries and commentaries. Examples of this genre include the major prophetic books such as Isaiah, Jeremiah, Daniel, and Ezekiel, and the Minor Prophets such as Hosea, Amos, and Jonah.

3. *Poetic Literature*. Biblical poetry is similar to modern poetry in its use of description, symbols, and metaphor. One major difference, however, is that biblical poetry has a preference for the stylistic form of parallelism. Parallelism is that form of thought wherein the author intentionally contrasts or repeats concepts and phrases for effect. Poetry as a

form can be found in narratives (see Ex. 15:1–18 and Luke 1:46–55) and prophetic literature (see Isa. 66:1–3), but the clearest example is the book of Psalms.

4. *Wisdom Literature*. Wisdom literature typically contains collections of wise sayings, or proverbs, written in small units. Wisdom books often utilize literary devices like repetition and hyperbole to convey a specific principle that, when observed, will help the reader to live life skillfully. These principles are not promises, but general rules accumulated by wise teachers who have observed this world and have discerned what shapes a life that is pleasing to God. Proverbs and Ecclesiastes are good examples of this genre. The book of Job is also wisdom literature, but it presents an extended meditation on what is the wise response to suffering.

5. *Epistles*. An epistle is a letter written to a person or a group of people. Often these letters, though having a specific addressee, were circulated among various churches. Much of the New Testament features this genre, including Paul's epistles, Hebrews, James, 1 and 2 Peter, the three short letters by John, and Jude. Paul's letters, in particular, follow an "epistolary form" that mirror the forms of other ancient letters, such as address formulas (from [author] to [addressee]), formal greetings, wishes for well-being, the letter proper (with requests, commands, and updates), and salutations.

6. *Apocalyptic Literature*. The apocalyptic genre is characterized by revelations of future events, particularly as they relate to the end times. Some books are both apocalyptic and prophetic (Daniel, for example). Its name comes from the Greek work *apokalūptō*, which means to unveil or reveal something. These announcements are often given by an angel and the author acts as the recorder of these revelations. This genre typically uses symbols and fantastic imagery to describe these future events. Examples of this genre are Daniel and Revelation.

Scripture was not meant to be read as individually packaged, motivational sound bites. Because God inspired the authors of Scripture, the individual books all flow out of the larger story of how He is at work in His creation, revealing His plan to redeem, restore, and reconcile it to Himself. This means that any verse, passage, chapter, or book of the Bible needs to be contextualized into this larger, interconnected story.

Another way to help with contextualizing a passage is to look at parallel passages to the verse or chapter you are reading. Seeing how the author drew on, quoted, or mirrored the ideas of other biblical writers can help you grasp the meaning of the passage. Most Bibles include verse references to these parallel passages in the margins. If you are using an online Bible, these parallel passages are usually hyperlinked.

God always reveals Himself within the conventions and

restrictions of a specific historical and cultural context. This means that knowing more about the author, the time period, key figures, key nations, local geography, and cultural practices can all be important tools in understanding the meaning of the text.

Yet at the core of God's redemptive plan for this world is the sending of Christ, the Messiah. It is Christ, as the incarnate Word of God, who most fully reveals God to His creation. As a result, to fully understand the meaning of any Scripture, we must understand it in light of Christ. This means that every passage of Scripture anticipates, points to, and reveals Christ. Reading this way is called a christological reading of Scripture. The key to understanding the Bible is to see how it relates to Jesus Christ. Christ is *the* key to the Scriptures (see John 5:39).

John the Baptist made that clear when he said of Jesus, "Behold, the Lamb of God who takes away the sin of the world!" (John 1:29). What John was saying is that the entire sacrificial system of the Mosaic Law pointed forward to Jesus. Today, the entire New Testament points backward to Jesus. He is the living, incarnate Word of God. As you observe the text, find Jesus in your passage; you will be on the right track to its meaning.

Something very exciting happens when you begin to rightly interpret the truth of God's Word and see its connection to Jesus. When God opens the truth of His Word to your understanding, your heart will burn with new excitement and insight, which will be reflected in your preaching. In Nehemiah 8, when the people of God heard His Word as it was read to them, they threw a party because they were full of joy at understanding the Scriptures. Part of your role as a pastor is to help your congregants fall in love with Scripture and its Author—and hopefully to the degree that they want to throw a party due to their excitement of understanding God and His Word!

God the Holy Spirit wants to guide you into "all the truth" in your preaching (John 16:13). He doesn't just want you to deliver the teaching of the Word, but to also be *in* the Word. He wants to make His Word burn in your heart because when you apply what the Holy Spirit of God is teaching you, your ministry will be changed by the power of His transforming Word.

CHAPTER FOUR

PRESENTATION

❖

A common struggle for pastors is crafting and presenting their sermons in a way that provides relevant application to the hearers. When your message fails to communicate applications and achieve relevancy in the lives of the hearers, much of what you have said will become lost in translation.

The goal of relevancy is twofold: to demonstrate the contemporary nature of Scripture, which speaks to the needs of the audience, and to reveal God in understandable terms, which lead people to the Bible to seek God's will for their lives. The goal of presenting an applicable sermon is to provide the necessary actionable items that will produce steps toward life transformation. When pastors and preachers continuously fail to connect Scripture to the lives of their congregants, they miss these two marks. Since the Word of God is powerful and relevant, our preaching must help others see that truth.

The Bible was written to real people with real needs. We can see how God chooses to be relevant in Scripture through His choice to speak in human terms and to make Himself known to us through the incarnation. We also see how Jesus was relevant in His teaching by often speaking in parables and analogies, which related to the environment of the times in which He lived.

The apostles also spoke in relevant terminology and topics. For example, Paul frequently used phrases related to athletics, thus setting the Christian life in terms that the contemporary culture could easily identify with. He spoke of Christianity as if it were running a race (1 Cor. 9:24; Gal. 2:2; 5:7; 2 Tim. 4:7). Wrestling with sin was like boxing (1 Cor. 9:26). Waging spiritual warfare was akin to a Roman soldier heading into battle (Eph. 6:10–18). His illustrations and topics were always punctuated with relevancy, which not only caught a reader's attention, but also kept it.

When discussing or teaching on relevancy in preaching, I often come across those who don't know whether relevancy is all that important. After all, isn't the Word of God already relevant? Why would I as a pastor need to make it relevant? Well, if the Bible is relevant already, then a preacher should complement the Scripture through expressing that relevancy in his sermon.

Another objection I've heard is that it's the job of the Holy Spirit, not preachers, to apply the Word. But it is also the job of the Holy Spirit to save sinners, yet He expects you and I to witness (Acts 1:8). In fact, it's also the job of the Holy Spirit to comfort believers in their distress, yet we are told to "comfort one another" (1 Thess. 4:18). Yes, it is the job of the Holy Spirit to teach and reveal divine truth, yet He has also called you to preach God's Word. Thus, the Holy Spirit works with and through human agencies, not apart from them, to accomplish relevancy.

Pastor, irrelevant sermons—that is, those that have no bearing on people's lives—fall short of biblical preaching. The flipside of that is true as well. Entirely "relevant" sermons—those that seek simply to accommodate people's interests without any biblical anchoring—are not preaching either. That's called a lecture or an inspirational talk and not a sermon. Yes, you want to get your audience to laugh and cry at times because authentic emotion is part of life transformation. But you want to be careful not to make such emotional responses the end goal. Illustrations, which often evoke emotions, should illustrate. If they become the centerpiece of your sermon rather than helpful ways to unpack the biblical truth being taught, then they are not serving the right purpose.

Never throw in illustrations simply for a reaction when they have nothing to do with what you're preaching on. When you do, your sermon ends up being one story on top of another with no explanation or exegetical application. While such a tactic may draw people to the preacher, it won't draw people to Scripture—or God. Always remember that relevancy must connect to the Bible itself.

HINDRANCES TO RELEVANCY

There are several things that hinder a preacher from being relevant. People sometimes listen poorly. Their minds wander. People decide quickly where to focus their attention, and like it or not, you are competing for the minds and ears of your listeners. This is the digital media, 280-character, 15-second Instagram story culture that we live in today. If you want your congregants to track with you longer than fifteen seconds, you're going to need to work hard at making what you are saying relevant enough to gain and retain their attention. The attention of your audience cannot be assumed. It must be won. Never assume that everyone is simply panting to hear what you have to say. Keep your sermon intriguing and interesting without neglecting the biblical point.

What's more, people often think in pictures. They react in pictures, visually. While not everyone does this, a good number of people do. And because we are so inclined to think visually in our day, sitting down to listen to a long sermon can be challenging—unless that sermon has something to do with them.

Another hindrance to relevant preaching is sheer laziness on the pastor's part. Just as it takes work to determine the meaning of a biblical text, it also takes work to effectively communicate that message to your audience. There's no getting around the need to roll up your sleeves and do the work.

Another hindrance is poor exegesis. As we've seen, part of the exegetical process consists of properly identifying the situation of the biblical author's audience as well as the audience you are addressing today. I like to call this "dual exegesis." A preacher has to both exegete the Scripture and exegete his contemporary culture. Remember, you are positioned between two worlds. You have the Bible in one hand and the digital news on your smartphone in another. You've got to read both and interpret both in order to draw out the relevancy between the two.

Pastors are also hindered in their ability to be relevant by the lack of significant social interaction. If you are going to speak to people's hearts and lives in your sermons, you must interact with them. You must not make assumptions about your members, but rather get to know them personally so you can make your messages applicable to them.

There's also a worldview issue that hinders relevancy. Theology that intersects only with philosophy—and not sociology or ethics—will not be sensitive to the needs of people. People have questions regarding their social realities and ethical dilemmas. Your listeners want to know what the Bible says about work, raising kids who won't behave, single parenting, addictions, and more. This is why it is critical that you preach from a kingdom-centric worldview. Since the kingdom is the comprehensive rule of God, then His kingdom agenda can be applied to every area of life through your preaching.

INGREDIENTS OF RELEVANCY

Continually seek to implement appropriate illustrations into your sermons. If illustrations don't come easily to you, you need to practice so that incorporating them into your sermons eventually becomes natural to you. One of the ways to do this is to change your mindset. Decide that your sermon is not finished until it has been made relevant. You could purchase an illustration book to help in this regard. But also look for life lessons that the Holy Spirit brings to your mind. Pastor, everything (and everyone) around you is a potential illustration.

When I taught the preaching course at Dallas Theological Seminary and the subject of illustrations came up, I always challenged my students to name anything they wanted, and I would turn it into an illustration in less than a minute. They would throw out things like a camera. To which I would respond that a camera captures snapshots of our lives for viewing later. Similarly, when we all stand before God at the judgment seat of Christ, He is going to play back the tape of our lives, so to speak. You and God will sit in your private view booth, of sorts, to determine your reward based on what that camera reveals. I'm not some "illustration robot"; I have *learned* to think illustratively. Pastor, you must learn to think this way too.

In addition to changing your mindset and using contemporary illustrations, developing creative sermon titles helps make a relevant sermon. Such titles can invoke interest in your message and couch the sermon in a relevant frame of a mind for the listener before you even begin. This past summer, I preached every Wednesday night on a series called "Hot Topics." These were the topics that our culture debated, argued over, posted on via social media, and more. Topics included gender confusion, the #MeToo movement, race wars, and a plethora of other delicate yet relevant topics to spend time on through preaching and through question-and-answer times. Thus, the title "Hot Topics" set the tone for the messages.

When I preached on Hebrews 12, I titled my sermon "A Whole Lot of Shaking Going On" because the passage is about God's unshakeable kingdom in the midst of a shaken society. As I mentioned previously, I preached on manhood earlier this year and rather than title it "Biblical Manhood," I called it "Adam, Where You At?" Captivating titles generate interest and set the tone of the series. In creating a sermon title, I want to signal to people that I am intentionally seeking to make the sermon itself attention-grabbing and interesting.

THE DYNAMICS OF DELIVERY

Delivery also relates to relevancy. Delivery refers to those vocal and visual behaviors shaped by and subject to the main point and its implications, which enable the communicator to convey the message to others. *How* you say something is just as important as *what* you say. A good message poorly presented hinders reception. Delivery involves determining how you are going to communicate what you have prepared so that it is effective and relies on a number of factors.

First, is *presence*. Your presence must never distract from your message, whether it be what you wear or how you stand, whether you fumble with your notes or your shoe is untied. A pastor must always focus on personal presence. A negative distraction might be a crooked tie or slouched shoulders. But conversely, positive aspects (taken to the extreme) can also distract such as being too flamboyant in your clothing or mannerisms. You want how you look and how you carry yourself to complement your message, not to distract from it.

In your delivery, you also need to pay attention to your *volume*. Speaking loudly enough for your congregation to hear is critical. However, speaking too loudly can turn people off. Every great presenter varies his or her volume in order to keep the audience engaged. If you talk in a monotone delivery style, people will tune out. Thus, your voice should be used strategically—to emphasize a point, regain attention after a long teaching portion, or for any number of reasons. Just as you would turn off a movie that had only one scene, your congregants desire variety in how you deliver your message throughout the entirety of the message. Like the plot of a quality movie, your sermon should help steer your listeners toward the overarching principles and main point.

Preachers, your job is to make sure your point is clear. Use your voice to do so. The *pitch*—the highness or lowness of the sound of your voice—is to be commensurate with your point. You can't be making a passionate, life-changing point without passion in your voice. If it's a passionate point, it ought to be passionately presented within the context of your own personality. How can you talk about the glory of heaven with no glory in your voice? Or how you can talk about how terrible hell is going to be with no fire in your own voice? Your pitch must fit the point your making.

Equally important is your *pace*, how fast or slow you speak. Your pace should be fast enough to be engaging, but slow enough to be understood. When you're speaking on a painful subject, you normally don't want to talk fast because you want to empathize with people. Consider yourself. When you are hurting, you want someone who will speak slowly, calmly, and with empathy. As a preacher, your pace must match your point as well as the emotions that are being raised by what you say.

Your pace also must be used to emphasize what is being said. It sets the mood. Intentionally placed pauses give your audience time to let a principle or thought sink in. A pause may just be a second or two, but when done well, it helps establish a mood. Delivering a sermon well involves setting, maintaining, and directing the atmospheric mood throughout the entirety of the message. The mood of your listeners must be in cadence with your own. If the message is about fear or anxiety, people ought to pick that up subconsciously in the mood as well as in what you say. If the message is about pain, they ought to experience that to some degree too. If it's about joy, they ought to pick up exuberance from you. If you don't feel it first, you will fail to find a way for them to feel it too.

Scripture is replete with moods. Feelings abound on the pages of God's Word, and any feeling imaginable is reflected in Scripture. There's intrigue, fear, love, passion, pain, loss, grief, anger, and so much more. God's Word is a living drama. Flowing throughout the pages of Scripture are the moods of the people of Scripture and of those who penned Scripture. Your role as the preacher is to identify and empathize with these moods in order to communicate them effectively.

In recent years, there has been a greater emphasis on using creative tools as you preach. These are known as *object lessons*. For example, an object lesson I use to demonstrate a person's value to God is a one hundred dollar bill. When I crumple the bill, throw it on the ground, and stomp on it, the congregation still concurs that the bill is valuable, just as valuable as before. I will then typically ask someone if they want it, and many people will come forward to get it. This provides a visual illustration of our value before God. Jesus used object lessons in His teaching regularly, whether it was the cup at the well in Samaria or the fig tree or the coin in the fish's mouth, these tangible items explain a point in a way that is memorable (John 4:7–38; Mark 11:12–14; Matt. 17:24–27). Don't be afraid to incorporate them into your sermon but also be mindful (as you should be in using other illustrations) not to rely on them entirely or have them detract from the truths at hand.

Eye contact during your delivery is another useful way of gaining and maintaining attention. Again, people ought to feel the truth that you are preaching and not just hear it. One way people feel is through regular eye contact.

The Word of God changes lives, reverses circumstances, and is a powerful source of blessing. Your role as the preacher is to appropriately prepare and then effectively proclaim God's truth in such a way that draws your listeners closer to the heart of God Himself. Ultimately, life change results from the Holy Spirit's development of a person's life, but God has both designed and called preachers to communicate His Word to provide the greatest opportunity for life change to take place. Pastor, preach the Word—in season and out—so that heaven will be filled with those lives who God calls through your faithful study, application, prayer, and preaching.

PREACHING
RESOURCES

———————◆———————

CREATING A MASTER PREACHING CALENDAR

———————— ◆ ————————

A master preaching calendar is a projected plan (up to six months or more) for preaching that includes a date, passage, and title for each sermon (ultimately, it should include the main idea to go with each title). It is assumed that the individual sermons will be clustered in a collection of varying lengths, organized around a book of the Bible or a common topic.

YOUR PREACHING CALENDAR
SHOULD REFLECT YOUR ROLES

Your preaching calendar should reflect your responsibilities to both instruct and motivate. Remember, as a preacher, you are a teacher. And the single most important emphasis you can have as a teacher is the grace of God. Without an understanding of God's grace, no one can be what God has created him to be. The master preaching calendar should reflect this understanding.

Preacher, you are also a shepherd. As such, you must know (1) where God wants you to go in your preaching schedule, (2) why God wants you to go there, and (3) how God wants you to get there. Only when you know where you are headed, why you are headed there, and how to get there can you effectively lead God's people. Make sure your preaching calendar reflects your sense of God-given direction. In addition to this, be sure that your master preaching calendar reflects your values as a preacher and pastor.

STEPS TO CREATING A MASTER PREACHING CALENDAR

1. Avoid last-minute panic. Last-minute panic affects the quality of preaching and the nerves of the preacher; it can be easily avoided by working ahead. Long-term planning ensures a good quality sermon and peace of mind.

2. Lay the groundwork for planning a master preaching calendar. The main ingredients here are: (1) spending time regularly with the Lord in Scripture and prayer; (2) spending time with people in your congregation so you know their needs; (3) spending time in society so you know not only the needs of society, but also what pressures from society your congregants may be facing.

3. Follow a planned process for developing a master preaching calendar. I like to set aside at least a weekend every few months to focus on this process. Before you get away, arrange for someone else to preach in your absence. I believe it's important to get away from home and your normal routine so you can focus on one primary task: prayerfully and dependently planning the proclamation of God's Word. If your family can allow you to work effectively, take them along and give them a break from their routine as well. Attempt to have your church cover at least part of the travel and lodging costs.

Here are important steps to follow:

- Select and arrange for the place where you will work.
- Gather and bring all resources you will need to prepare your plan.
- Lay out your daily schedule and set your goals so you know what you are seeking to accomplish before you go.
- Spend part of each day:

  « restoring and refreshing your walk with God
  « exegeting Scripture
  « reading and thinking
  « exercising

- Prepare at least two to three months in advance to get the most out of your planning.

- Determine which books of the Bible, biblical themes, and contemporary issues you will teach on during that planned period.

It's important that you always think about the minds and needs of your congregation during this process. And as you begin this process, write down the needs of your people. Be sure that these needs inform your instructional and motivational aims. And be intentional about how you will meet the needs of the people and achieve these aims.

ADVANTAGES TO DEVELOPING
A MASTER PREACHING CALENDAR

Perhaps the most obvious advantage to creating a master preaching calendar is that it allows you to see the complete picture of your pulpit ministry—at least over a three- to six-month period (or even longer). Not only that, a calendar promotes synergy between your work in the pulpit and teaching done elsewhere in the church. If the majority of adults are doing a Bible book study, you may want to offer a different diet from the pulpit.

Another incredible advantage is that it protects you from preaching too many times on the same subject. Your memory will fool you, and developing a preaching calendar, as well as reviewing past ones, will keep you preaching on fresh texts and topics. It also helps maintain variety in the scope of messages and series lengths. You are more likely to include topical studies as well as book studies and should also be able to see at a glance where your longer or shorter series will fall.

Logistically speaking, it also saves time. Much time can be wasted searching for a text instead of working on a specific text. Also, your study one week should contribute to your study for the next week if it is part of a series. On a related note, a preaching calendar offsets interruptions. If you know exactly where you are going four or five weeks from now, you can tolerate the interruptions easier—and all pastors get interruptions.

I find that creating a preaching calendar gives me peace of mind. A track has been laid so that I know what text I will be preaching on.

Creating and following a calendar also drives the preacher to his study. Since you know where you are going to be in the text, you can dive right in. By having a calendar, you know what you have to do, and knowing that helps force you to execute.

A preaching calendar also helps a pastor maintain a balanced ministry from the pulpit by planning when outside speakers, films, or groups will be ministering to the people. If someone requests time to address the people, a planned pulpit ministry either allows for it or gives some rationale why the person cannot be included in the schedule.

I also find that a preaching calendar makes it easier to schedule messages on the basis of goals or objectives. If you know many unsaved people will be present at a Sunday evening baptismal time, then your objective of evangelism may help dictate what is preached.

GUIDELINES FOR CREATING AN ANNUAL MASTER PREACHING CALENDAR

If you want to create an annual preaching calendar, allow enough time to preach adequately through a designed series. The book of Romans, for example, will require more than one quarter (13 weeks) to preach on effectively.

Be careful about staying in one book too long. One year devoted to Colossians is too long. Sometimes we wrongly assume that everyone is as interested in methodical analysis as we are.

Be flexible! Do not hesitate to interrupt a series for a timely message. The holiday seasons or special days may be good interruptions of your current series.

Set up a long-range program for preaching through the major books of the Bible. This will help ground the people in biblical theology. You will put the emphasis where God puts the emphasis.

Seasonal series can be helpful periodically. For example,

preaching on prophecies of Christ's first coming prior to Christmas, or a series on Jesus Christ from Christmas to Easter, or featuring the home from Mother's Day through Father's Day.

In determining the series you will preach throughout the year, survey your congregation to determine their needs. Be intentional about using questionnaires and making pastoral visits, for example. These help you understand the needs of the church. The results may indicate that you need to address a series of messages on missions, fellowship, or prayer, for example. It is also wise to solicit suggestions from your leaders in the congregation. You will need to open the door of your office—literally and figuratively—for their suggestions. Otherwise, they likely will not provide them. Your board can be extremely helpful by giving you a different perspective, too.

Keep in mind that it is wise to address the trends of the times. You may need to address, for example, what the Bible says about immorality among leaders, how believers today respond to the racial crisis, and how active believers should be in the political arena.

Creatively establish your annual master pulpit plan. If you have just accepted a pastorate, why not start with a series of three messages on expectations:

1. What does God expect of your pastor?
2. What does God expect of His people?

3. What does God expect of the pastor and people working together?

Review previous calendars before establishing the new pulpit plan. This protects continuity in the pulpit. It also can be a time of evaluation of performance in light of goals.

Use variety within the bounds of propriety. Do not restrict the people to constantly listening to only you. You will need to determine how much of the public pulpit work should be done by you. Films, panels, question and answer, drama, cantatas, children's church, youth, missionaries, Bible conference, family conference, and many more are possible formats and, at times, should be included.

Select a cross-section of your congregation and have them regularly input ideas as to topics that should be addressed when the corporate church meets.

Balance Old Testament studies with New Testament messages so your people have a good understanding of the Bible as a whole. This means you should not shy away from some biblical literature that may be more difficult for you to prepare a sermon on.

When it is warranted, do not hesitate to insert a message that has not been scheduled in the yearly plan. And when you plan the calendar, as well as when you depart from the calendar, make prayer a priority.

CREATING A SERMON

———————— ◆ ————————

Here are simple questions to keep in mind as you prepare your sermon.

PERSONAL

Have you adequately prayed for yourself? For your members? And for your message?

Are you excited about your message?

Have you sought to apply the main principles to your own life?

INTRODUCTION

Have you given it due attention?

Does it touch a real felt need, either directly or indirectly?

Does it orient the audience to the subject? To the big idea? Or to your first main point?

Is it the right length (time)?

What is the purpose of this sermon/lesson?

- To teach a Bible doctrine (Justification, God, etc.)?
- To educate the believers about their Christian position?
- To challenge people to take a biblical issue seriously?
- To motivate the people for an action?
- To settle theological disputes (apologetic)?
- To proclaim the gospel to non-Christians?
- To encourage with biblical blessings, etc.?

The "Three Is" of an Introduction

1. *Interest:* Will you generate interest in the first few sentences? Put another way, will listeners think to themselves, *This speaker is worth listening to?*

2. *Involvement:* Will you touch on some need or curiosity in the first few paragraphs? Will listeners think to themselves, *This message is worth listening to?*

3. *Information:*

   Focus: a crisp statement of the big idea (deductive) or of the subject (inductive)

   Context: the biblical background or setting where the same idea or subject/question comes up (but without mentioning book, chapter, or verse)

   Preview: how the message will unfold, what's to come,

how to listen, the road map of what's ahead

Passage: book, chapter, and verse

(Note: Context and preview can be reversed)

STRUCTURE

Is the development of the sermon clear?

Is the overall outline structure clear?

Does the sermon have a big idea?

- Can you state it?
- Must the idea be proven?
- Should the idea be explained (illustrated)?

Is the message faithful to the text?

Is the immediate as well as far-reaching context of the passage being honored? For example, is this sermon in harmony with the overall theme of the biblical book?

Does the fruit of exegesis appear in this sermon?

Does the text dictate the flow of thought in your message?

Does analysis of the text appear accurate and complete?

Is this message theologically sound?

Have you done an exegetical outline? An expositional outline? A homiletical outline? (Note: More info on this in "Types of Outlines.")

Are the transitions clear? Do they review content from a previous section?

Is there a logical or psychological link between the points?

Do the main points relate back to the main idea?

Are the sub-points clearly related to their main points?

CONCLUSION

Does the sermon build to a climax? What is it?

Is there an adequate summary of ideas? How?

Are there effective appeals or suggestions for action?

Does the sermon suggest concrete application(s)?

What is the one thing you want your listeners to carry home?

Q & A ON PREACHING

———————— ◆ ————————

Do you take your manuscript or your outline to the pulpit to preach?

I do not use a manuscript; it's a preference of mine. Some people do, and that's great for them. I outline my sermon. But even then, I may not use it in the pulpit. When I do use it, however, I don't use the full outline because I never want to get locked into something written. I want the Spirit to be able to move me where He wants me to go in my preaching. That's why I prepare an outline but don't always use it.

When you preach on a holiday or a Sunday near a holiday, do you craft your whole sermon around the holiday or simply mention the holiday briefly?

It depends. Sometimes I connect the holiday to the sermon if the message allows for it, or I take a break in the current series I'm preaching and dedicate the whole sermon to the holiday. For example, a lot of people are traveling at Christmas. They are thinking about kids and toys and gifts and family and more. It's difficult to preach a sermon in a series on the Sunday before Christmas and on the Sunday right after Christmas. So I generally take that whole time to focus on the holiday season.

What is a major pitfall of using a preaching calendar?

The calendar can become inflexible, and you may not recognize major events that take place in your community or in the larger society if you are focused so much on what you've already set in place. Change whatever you're preaching on when something like 9/11 happens. It's amazing that some preachers will keep preaching their series when nobody's thinking about what they're talking about in light of what just happened in the country, city, or community. You have to stay relevant to where people are. Once the calendar becomes inflexible, then you're not really justifying its purpose.

How do you handle being invited to speak in a revival setting?

First, I consider whether the group that has invited me has a theme or general idea they want me to preach on. If so, try to meet their needs. And usually when doing a series, don't try to create something new if you're still having to prepare for your own congregation. For the sake of time, reuse something you've already preached, and make it relevant to the revival group. The Synoptic Gospels are written as the same general story—Matthew, Mark, and Luke. But they tell the same stories from different perspectives because they're reaching different audiences respectively. If the revival group leaves it up to you to decide the theme, then preach what you are passionate about because that will be a blessing to the people.

How do you re-orient yourself to your prepared sermon outline when something breaks the flow of the sermon or service?

First of all, I ask the Holy Spirit to guide me back on track. That's His job, anyway—to bring the truth to our minds, just as He did for the apostles. There was a big gap between when Jesus was with them on earth and when it was time for them to write. The gap was closed by the work of the Holy Spirit. If it's a graphic thing, and everyone is distracted, ask the people to join you in prayer. That way they become participants and can see the work of the Spirit right there on stage.

In terms of planning, what do you do when you're not dealing with the same audience consistently?

More of your preparation should be focused on giving individual messages rather than working through series, unless the series is such that each message could stand alone. Hopefully you've accumulated individual messages, which means you can rotate them because the group is rotating. So don't get locked down. If the group is different each time you preach, and that's what God has called you to, then you just make each message self-contained and not dependent on what came before it or what will come after it.

Do you reuse outlines?

Peter said, "I bring these things to your remembrance." A principle here leads me to believe that it's perfectly okay to reuse content to remind people of things they've already learned or heard, so long as you're doing it with freshness. In other words, you don't say, "Well, I'm going to reuse this series, so I'm not even going to look at it or study it until Sunday morning when I get up to preach it," because there is no freshness in that. You still need the fresh work of the Spirit, even if it's an old outline. You want to go over it again. Is there anything new that the congregation is going through? Is there anything new on the subject so you can take an old outline and still make it a fresh presentation?

How do you approach preaching in multiple services back to back?

There's always a difference between the two services because the Spirit does something a little different in both because the people in each service are different. It's all right, and even good for your own sake, to preach from the same basic outline, preach on the same basic theme and same basic Scripture passage. But the flow of your sermons will no doubt be slightly different from each other. The audience is a little different, so you plan to preach the same thing, but the Spirit has freedom to make little adjustments along the way.

What about preachers seeking to manually or arbitrarily manufacture spiritual results rather than leaving the results to the Holy Spirit?

If by "manufacturing" results we mean using illegitimate means to get a response or trying to make something happen that it is apparent God is not making happen, then you're trying to play God at that point. But if we mean seeking to make the sermon apply to the hearers through the use of persuasive speaking approaches, that's totally legitimate. If I were to try to coerce a response, the response would not be a God-driven one because it would not be a heart response. God wants the heart, not the feet with no heart. He doesn't want you standing up on the outside and sitting down on the inside.

What's your view on giving an invitation to walk to the front of the sanctuary after the sermon in response to what God has done in hearers' hearts?

I give it sometimes. It depends on whether that is the best way for someone to respond to the sermon. I don't need the same people walking up front every week. If I'm giving an evangelistic message, I'll call people forward because we want to be able to share with them, witness to them, and give them material to read. If the message is not evangelistic, such as a sermon on addictions of any kind, I'll call people who are facing addictions to come forward. But sometimes, I call people to make a response right in their seat, and I'm not trying to get them to come forward. You always want a response, but the response doesn't always have to be walking forward. The response can be a heart response. It could be a decision for a father to start having devotions with his family. Walking forward doesn't get him to start doing devotions with his family. Going home and having devotions with his family is what needs to happen. So coming forward is one means, but it's not the only means in which people respond to God.

Is it good to give an invitation to accept the gospel at a funeral?
At a funeral, especially where a significant number of non-believers are typically present, you always want to give an opportunity to understand the gospel and respond to it. It may not be appropriate to invite people forward to be prayed for. You need to keep in mind that flow of service. Because of that, you might want to include an invitation on the back of the program, a number to call or a website to visit if a person wants to know more about the gospel.

What general advice do you have for aspiring preachers?
Commit yourself early "to study the law of the Lord and to practice it, and to teach His statutes and ordinances in Israel" (Ezra 7:10). In other words, studying the Word, living the Word, meditating on the Word, so there's always a freshness to your preaching, conviction behind it, and a life that attests to it.

How do I apply fasting to the preaching process?

Fasting in the Bible was used when there was a particular need or there was a desire for God to do a special thing. I will fast when something unique is taking place. Fasting puts a fire under prayer and "heats it up" so to speak. In fasting, you deny the physical because you need more of the spiritual in this situation. Every year our church has a Solemn Assembly, a week of fasting, for the needs of our church.

TYPES OF OUTLINES

---◆---

SAMPLE EXEGETICAL OUTLINE

Matthew 28:16–20

Subject: Jesus' command to make disciples.

Complement: The responsibility of His people in this age.

Main Point: The content of Jesus' command to His followers is that they are to make disciples of all people.

1. The meaning of Christ's command to make disciples is to bring people into total conformity to His authority.

   - The goal of discipleship is the imitation of Christ (Matt. 10:24–25).
   - The cost of discipleship is rejection, persecution, and death (Matt. 10:28–39).
   - The scope of discipleship includes every area of life (1 Cor. 10:31).

2. The basis of Christ's command to make disciples because of the nature of His authority (Matt. 28:18).

- The meaning of Christ's authority is that it is the only one that is legitimate as opposed to the illegitimate claims of Satan.
- The foundation for Christ's legitimate authority is His resurrection from the dead that defeated the power of Satan.
- The scope of Christ's authority is universal in nature, extending to the comprehensive spheres of heaven and earth.
- The source of Christ's authority is God the Father.

3. The means by which Christ's disciples are made is threefold (vv. 19–20a).

- The first means by which disciples are made is through the dissemination of the gospel message to the world by His followers (Matt. 10:7).
- The second means by which disciples are made is in their public identification with the Triune God in every area of life as symbolized in baptism.
- The third means by which disciples are made is through the comprehensive instruction of all that Christ taught in order that lifestyles might change to visibly reflect His teachings.

4. The result of Christ's command to those who make disciples is that they will experience His unique personal presence and assistance as they are involved in the discipleship process (v. 20b).

- Christ promises His personal presence as the discipleship process is being carried out indicated by the use of the emphatic "I."
- Christ's special presence extends throughout the age of grace.
- Christ's special presence provides the power for the discipleship process.

SAMPLE EXPOSITIONAL OUTLINE

Matthew 28:16–20

Subject: Jesus' command to make disciples.

Complement: The responsibility of His people in this age.

Main Point: The content of Jesus' command to His followers is that they are to make disciples of all people.

1. Introduction

- The limitation of the Super Tuesday election to change the condition of your world
- The secularism of our age

- The nature of God's kingdom (Joshua and the captain of the Lord's army)
- The power of God's people (Abraham in Sodom)

(What then should be the goal of God's people today?)

- Main Point: Making disciples is the mission of the church.
- Background
  « Jesus makes an appointment after His Resurrection.
  « There are three groups present: the eleven, the five hundred, and all other believers through history, including us today.

2. Body

- The *perspective* for making disciples is total commitment to Christ (Matt. 10:24–39).
  « Discipleship means to live under the lordship of Christ.
  « Discipleship means to live for the glory of God.
  « Illustration: being drafted into the Army; the philosophy of Paul.

(From the *perspective* for making disciples we move to the *power*.)

- The *power* for making disciples is the authority of Christ (v. 18).
  - « This authority is comprehensive for this age.
  - « This authority is universal in its scope.
  - « This authority is supernatural in its nature.
  - « This authority is preparatory for the age that is to come.
  - « Illustration: the US invasion of Granada.

(From the *power* of making disciples we move to the *process*.)

- The *process* for making disciples is the threefold instruction of Christ (v. 19–20a).
  - « The process starts with public evangelism ("Go").
  - « Illustration: a huddle in a football game.
  - « The process is demonstrated through personal identification ("Baptism").
  - « The process is developed through practical instruction. ("Teaching").

(From the *process* for making disciples we conclude with the *prize*.)

- The *prize* for making disciples is the presence of Christ. (v. 20b)
  - « The prize is the personal presence of Christ.

« The prize is the permanent presence of Christ.

« The prize is the powerful presence of Christ.

« Illustration: the churches that are impacted are those making disciples, not just those having services.

3. Conclusion

- The church is a preview of coming attractions.

SAMPLE HOMILETICAL OUTLINE

Matthew 28:16–20

Subject: Jesus' command to make disciples.

Complement: The responsibility of His people in this age.

Main Point: The content of Jesus' command to His followers is that they are to make disciples of all people.

1. Introduction

- The limitation of the Super Tuesday elections.
- The secularism of our age.
- The nature of God's kingdom (Joshua and the captain of the Lord's army).
- The power of God's people (Abraham in Sodom).

(What then should be the goal of Christians today?)

- Main Point: Our job today is to make disciples of everyone.
- Background: We are part of the group that met with Jesus on the mountain.

2. Body

- First, we make disciples by bringing others to a total commitment to Christ (Matt. 10:24–39).
    « We must encourage them to make Christ Lord of their lives.
    « We must encourage them to reflect the character of God in every area of their lives.
    « We must encourage them to be willing to suffer for the cause of Christ.

Illustration: being drafted into the Army; the philosophy of Paul.

- Second, we make disciples by means of Christ's power working through us (v. 18).
    « His power is available for every Christian today.
    « His power is to be applied to every area of our lives.
    « His power is provided to us by God.

» His power prepares us for our future together with Him.

Illustration: the US invasion of Granada.

- Third, we make disciples by implementing Christ's procedures (v. 19–20a).
    » We must first be actively involved in evangelism.
    » Illustration: a huddle in a football game.
    » We must secondly help others to publicly display their faith.
    » We must finally teach others how they are to live by the Scriptures.

- Finally, we make disciples so they can experience the fullness of Christ's presence for themselves (v. 20b).
    » We will experience Christ's unique personal presence.
    » We will experience Christ's unique permanent presence.
    » We will experience Christ's unique powerful presence.

Illustration: the Christians that are having an impact are those making disciples, not just those that go to church.

3. Conclusion: Christians are a preview of coming attractions.

SAMPLE
SERMON OUTLINE

———————— ♦ ————————

SERMON TITLE: "REVIVE US AGAIN: NOW IS THE TIME FOR REVIVAL"

Suggested Passage: Haggai 1:2–11

Main Idea

Revival restores the priority of God's presence in the midst of His people.

Message Goal

For people to learn how to recognize God's warnings in our lives and to return our hearts and lives to our first love, where we will be completely satisfied in the Lord.

Sample Introduction

This message concerns something that, although often ignored, is very important to our walk with the Lord. There are times in our lives when God gives us warnings and tries to speak to us through life circumstances, but we don't hear Him or listen to His warning.

We are familiar with the function of an alarm clock or a siren. They serve to make us aware of something that needs our attention. God did this in Scripture many times when He spoke messages through the prophets of the Old Testament. Like a loud and intrusive noise, their message was not always expected or readily accepted, but it was necessary for the people.

Although a "minor prophet," Haggai sounded the warning to the Jews who had come back home to Israel after being in Babylonian captivity for 70 years. The problem was not that they were back, but that their priorities and lives reflected selfishness, not godliness. Haggai sounded the alarm to awaken everyone spiritually and point to lessons learned in the past. The people had been back from captivity for 15 years, yet the rebuilding of God's temple had been neglected, delayed, and eventually, ignored.

Haggai pinpointed the problem in verse 2: "Thus says the LORD of hosts, 'This people says, "The time has not come, even the time for the house of the LORD to be rebuilt."'" The temple had been destroyed when the Babylonians came many years earlier to take them into captivity. But when asked why they had not rebuilt, these Israelites who had come back to the land said, "We don't have time to rebuild the temple."

One of the reasons they didn't have time, or said they didn't have time, was because of opposition, as recorded in Ezra 4:1–5; 5:1–17.

But the main problem was that the people of Israel were satisfied without the temple because they were still carrying on with their religion. They were content to have God "in the vicinity" of their lives; they felt they didn't need Him "in the midst" of their lives, which is what the temple represented.

But there is a clear difference between a life that reflects true worship of God and one that just acknowledges God on the edge of life. Sometimes people need a stark reminder and an alarm to be rung so they can realize their sinfulness. This problem was not unique to the time of the prophets; it is a problem still plaguing Christians—even today.

We all recognize the need for a genuine revival, and we know that the alarm has been sounded. What do we need to do to course correct? How do we get to the position of putting God first in our lives? The answer is simple: we need a revival that will shake our comfort and put us in a right relationship with the Lord.

Sermon Points

1. Don't Be Satisfied Having God Just in the Vicinity

   - There is a difference between "God general" and "God specific"
     - « *General* means God is just there

« *Specific* means God is actively in your midst
« God is either on the outside or in the middle, right among you

- There is a difference in knowing of God and experiencing God
  « God is good to everybody
  « God is good to you in specific ways
  « You're either just acknowledging God or praising God

2. Your Life Will Indicate Whether You've Returned to God

- Treat the problem, not just the symptom
  « Israel's neglect of the temple was a warning light that signaled something was wrong
  « Don't just do part of the work
- A full 180-degree turn may be necessary
  « You must turn *from* your sin (Zech. 1:4)
  « You must also turn *to* the Lord (Zech. 1:6; Luke 15:17)

3. The Problem Is Often Our Priorities

- We make time for the things that matter most to us
  « Schedules are shuffled for what we consider top priority (Hag. 1:3–4)

« Time is not often "taken" as much as "made"

« A turn to God begins to happen when our schedules change

4. You Are Returning to God When He Takes Top Priority

- We don't reposition Him; we reposition ourselves
    - « God does not move or change who He is
    - « We must affix ourselves to Him as our steady point

- The Bible speaks often of Him being first
    - « Give the first part of everything to God (Deut. 26)
    - « Jesus Christ must have first place (Col. 1:18; Matt. 6:33)
    - « He wants to be our first love (Rev. 2:1–4)
    - « He is to have our best, not just our leftovers

5. God Demands Our "First Fruits"

- We often don't give to God our first fruits
    - « Most Christians give only a small percentage of "first fruits" they should be giving to God
    - « God sees our lack of giving as selfishness and stealing (Mal. 3:8)

- First fruits are more than money
    - « Energy and physical work are also fruits
    - « Focus and a clear mind are important fruits

6. We Must Consider Our Ways

- We must think about what we're doing for the Lord
    - « We must consider what the Lord says before acting (Mal. 1:7)
    - « Our efforts are in vain if we don't obey the Lord
- Our contentment can only be found in the Lord
    - « Paul agrees that the secret is contentment in the Lord (Phil. 4:11–12)
    - « Being constantly discontent is a sign of a needed heart change

SERMON ILLUSTRATIONS

Sounding The Alarm: I'm sure we all have alarm clocks sitting by our beds or on our phones that play a pivotal part of our daily routine. They are set the night before to alert us that it's time to wake up and start our day. They often go off during a very inconvenient time, but nonetheless they go off and help us get out of bed. We can try to ignore them, reset them, and even resist the call of the alarm, but they demand an immediate response.

God had alarm clocks, as it were, in the Bible: His prophets. Prophets were called in to wake up the people and alert them to something that God wanted them to hear. Just like our modern alarm clocks, the prophets were often unappreciated, and people tried to ignore or even resist them. But God wanted His people to be roused out of their cozy situation so He could accomplish something great with them.

Warning Lights: Our vehicles all have warning lights. These lights tell us that there is a bigger, deeper problem with our vehicle. The actual indicator light is not the problem, but it functions to tell us that something is not working properly. We can try to turn off the light, but that doesn't mean we've fixed the problem that can strand us. Many folks come to church knowing there is a warning light on in their lives, but they just want the light turned off for their convenience.

Making Time: It's amazing what happens to schedules during football season, especially here in the Dallas area. People always say they don't have time to do this or that, but all of a sudden at three o'clock on Sunday afternoon, people have three or four hours to watch the Dallas Cowboys. They will even rearrange or push back their schedules to accommodate watching the game.

BACKGROUND BIBLICAL HISTORY AND CULTURE

The Temple: The Old Testament temple was much more than just a building. It was the physical dwelling place of the glory of God, the representation of God among His people.

Old Testament Prophets: There are five "Major Prophets" in the Bible: Isaiah, Jeremiah, Lamentations, Ezekiel, and Daniel, and twelve "Minor Prophets": Hosea, Joel, Amos, Obadiah, Jonah, Micah, Nahum, Habakkuk, Zephaniah, Haggai, Zechariah, and Malachi. The Major Prophets are considered so because they are longer and their implications are more worldwide in nature. The Minor Prophets are called so because their books are shorter and their implications are more localized in their sweep. But all these books are important to read and are the inspired Word of God.

Persian Empire: (Hag. 1) Haggai prophesied during the Persian period of Jewish history. They started in Babylonian captivity under Nebuchadnezzar, but the Babylonian kingdom was taken over by the kingdom of the Persians and Medes. King Cyrus of Persia took Babylon, and the Jews were shortly thereafter allowed to begin returning home. The biblical books of Ezra, Nehemiah, Esther, Haggai, and Zechariah take place during this time period of about 200 years. Persian kings such as Cyrus, Darius, Xerxes, and

Artaxerxes played an important role as they allowed the Jews to return home to Jerusalem and God allowed favor to rest on His people, also fulfilling prophecy of their 70-year captivity followed by a return home.

NOTE: For the remaining outlines in the Revive Us Again series, please visit: https://go.tonyevans.org/dr-tony-evans-free-christian-sermon-notes where you will find the complete set plus a variety of other sermon outlines to assist you in your sermon preparation.

APPENDIX A

———— ◆ ————

RECOMMENDED RESOURCES

STUDY BIBLES

These are Bibles that include additional resources for study such as a topical index, topical concordance, maps, devotional reading, historical reading, and a variety of other unique insertions. Each study Bible is different.

Tony Evans Study Bible

Ryrie Study Bible

MacArthur Study Bible

Jeremiah Study Bible

CONCORDANCES AND PARALLEL REFERENCE WORKS

These resources include alphabetical listings of words (or topics) in the Bible, showing the biblical references where each occurs. This is a must in locating passages and in studying topics.

Young's Analytical Concordance of the Bible

Keyed to the KJV, its great strength is the analysis done which allows you to find every place a particular Greek or Hebrew word is located. Get the one by Eerdmans.

Strong's Concordance

Its great strength is the numbering system, which is tied in with many other study tools.

New American Standard Exhaustive Concordance

The only exhaustive concordance based on the New American Standard Bible. Every word in the NASB is listed (except words like "and," "the," etc.). References use the same numbering system as *Strong's Concordance*, thus making other word study tools accessible. It includes Hebrew and Greek dictionaries.

NIV Concordance

This is an excellent concordance, but only for the NIV Bible.

Treasury of Scripture Knowledge

This includes chronological data, concise chapter introductions, key word listings, illustrative notes, over 500,000 Scripture references, and parallel passages.

Nave's Topical Bible

Nave's is the best known and most comprehensive of the topical Bibles, containing over 20,000 topics and subtopics and 100,000 Scripture references.

Bible Dictionaries and Encyclopedias

These are alphabetical listings of people, places, things, events, and topics. They contain definitions, historical and cultural background material, outlines, and more.

New Bible Dictionary

This is the best one-volume Bible dictionary available today. Maps, diagrams, and charts expand and clarify the text.

Zondervan Pictorial Encyclopedia of the Bible

This excellent five-volume work covers in a well-rounded way significant issues relating to doctrines, themes, and biblical interpretation.

Unger's Bible Dictionary

With its 1,200 pages and 7,000 articles, *Unger's Bible Dictionary* has proved its value during ever-growing use as an authoritative reference work, encyclopedic in its scope.

New International Standard Bible Encyclopedia, Revised

This new edition, in four volumes, by G. W. Bromiley is fully revised, and the articles retained from the original edition have been completely updated (many completely rewritten) to take into account recent discoveries in archaeology and advances in other areas of biblical scholarship.

One-Volume Bible Commentaries

These are verse-by-verse explanations and interpretations of the Bible. They are necessarily brief.

Tony Evans Bible Commentary

The Bible Knowledge Commentary, Old Testament and *The Bible Knowledge Commentary, New Testament*

These helpful volumes are written by the Dallas Theological Seminary faculty.

Wycliffe Bible Commentary

The New Bible Commentary, Revised

Thoroughly revised and updated, this work provides good exposition available that is often difficult to find in a one-volume commentary.

Moody Bible Commentary

MacArthur Bible Commentary

Multi-Volume Bible Commentaries

These provide pastors and other Bible students with comprehensive and scholarly tools for the exposition of the Scriptures and the teaching and proclamation of their message.

The Expositor's Bible Commentary

> This series of volumes, based on NIV, provides pastors and other Bible students with a comprehensive and scholarly tool for the exposition of the Scriptures and the teaching and proclamation of their message.

Tyndale Old Testament and New Testament Commentaries

> This series does much of the same that the Expositor's Bible Commentary does.

The Wiersbe Bible Commentary

The Grace New Testament Commentary

BIBLE DOCTRINE

These resources provide systematic presentations of biblical truth about God, the Bible, Jesus, the Holy Spirit, man, salvation, the church, and the future.

Theology You Can Count On by Tony Evans

A Survey of Bible Doctrine by Charles Ryrie

Major Bible Themes by Lews Sperry Chafer, revised by John F. Walvoord

Basic Theology by Charles Ryrie

Moody Handbook of Theology by Paul Enns

The Grace Soteriology by David R. Anderson

Final Destiny by Joseph Dillow

The Kingdom Agenda by Tony Evans

BIBLE HANDBOOKS

These are gold mines of all kinds of helpful information about the Bible and related subjects such as archaeology, geography, and history, as well as notes and outlines of the Bible itself.

The New Unger's Bible Handbook. This is an excellent work; get it!

What the Bible is All About by Henrietta Mears

BIBLE SURVEYS

These surveys provide historical, geographical, political, and archaeological background as well as outlines for each book. They also cover the origin, date and place of writing, content, outline, emphasis, characters, and special features of each book of the Bible.

A Popular Survey of the Old Testament by Norman Geisler

New Testament Survey by Merrill C. Tenney

BIBLE ATLASES

These include maps of Bible lands, showing where the various events took place and giving helpful background information.

Moody Atlas of the Bible

This resource is new, conservative, and extremely helpful.

The Macmillan Bible Atlas

This is produced by excellent cartographers (map makers) who are Jewish and somewhat liberal, so one must be careful of their bias.

WORD STUDIES

Vine's Expository Dictionary of Old and New Testament Words

This is a one-volume reference guide for both Hebrew and Greek words. No knowledge of Greek and Hebrew is required. It sometimes makes too much out of roots and component parts of words but is still helpful.

New International Dictionary of New Testament Theology

This is a three-volume work of detailed study. Knowledge of Greek is not essential.

Theological Wordbook of the Old Testament
> This is a two-volume resource keyed to *Strong's Concordance*. You must have *Strong's* or know Hebrew to use this.

DEVOTIONAL AND SPIRITUAL LIFE

These resources provide a wealth of material, old and new, designed to encourage spiritual living.

Time to Get Serious by Tony Evans

Balancing the Christian Life by Charles Ryrie

The Pursuit of God by A. W. Tozer

Knowing God by J. I. Packer

Loving God by Chuck Colson

The Kingdom Agenda Devotional by Tony Evans

ELECTRONIC RESOURCES

Blue Letter Bible

Logos Bible Software

APPENDIX B

———————— ◆ ————————

MINISTRY OVERVIEW

The Urban Alternative (TUA) equips, empowers, and unites Christians to impact *individuals, families, churches,* and *communities* through a thoroughly kingdom agenda worldview. In teaching truth, we seek to transform lives.

The core cause of the problems we face in our personal lives, homes, churches, and societies is a spiritual one; therefore, the only way to address it is spiritually. We've tried a political, social, economic, and even a religious agenda.

It's time for a **Kingdom agenda**.

The Kingdom agenda can be defined as the visible manifestation of the comprehensive rule of God over every area of life. The unifying central theme throughout the Bible is the glory of God and the advancement of His kingdom. The conjoining thread from Genesis to Revelation—from beginning to end—is focused on one thing: God's glory through advancing God's kingdom.

When you do not have that theme, the Bible becomes disconnected stories that are great for inspiration but seem to be unrelated in purpose and direction. The Bible exists to share God's movement in history toward the establishment and expansion of His kingdom highlighting the connectivity throughout which is the kingdom. Understanding that increases the relevancy of this several-thousand-year-old manuscript to your day-to-day living, because the kingdom is not only then, it is now.

The absence of the kingdom's influence in our personal and family lives, churches, and communities has led to a deterioration in our world of immense proportions:

- People live segmented, compartmentalized lives because they lack God's kingdom worldview.
- Families disintegrate because they exist for their own satisfaction rather than for the kingdom.
- Churches are limited in the scope of their impact because they fail to comprehend that the goal of the church is not the church itself, but the kingdom.

- Communities have nowhere to turn to find real solutions for real people who have real problems because the church has become divided, ingrown, and unable to transform the cultural landscape in any relevant way.

The kingdom agenda offers us a way to see and live life with a solid hope by optimizing the solutions of heaven. When God—and His rule—is no longer the final and authoritative standard under which all else falls, order and hope leaves with Him. But the reverse of that is true as well: as long as you have God, you have hope. If God is still in the picture, and as long as His agenda is still on the table, it's not over.

Even if relationships collapse, God will sustain you. Even if finances dwindle, God will keep you. Even if dreams die, God will revive you. As long as God—and His rule—is still the overarching rule in your life, family, church, and community, there is always hope.

Our world needs the King's agenda. Our churches need the King's agenda. Our families need the King's agenda. In many major cities, there is a loop that drivers can take when they want to get somewhere on the other side of the city, but don't necessarily want to head straight through downtown. This loop will take you close enough to the city so that you can see its towering buildings and skyline, but not close enough to actually experience it.

This is precisely what we, as a culture, have done with God. We have put Him on the "loop" of our personal, family, church, and community lives. He's close enough to be at hand should we need Him in an emergency, but far enough away that He can't be the center of who we are.

We want God on the "loop," not the King of the Bible who comes downtown into the very heart of our ways. Leaving God on the "loop" brings about dire consequences as we have seen in our own lives and with others. But when we make God and His rule the centerpiece of all we think, do or say, it is then that we will experience Him in the way He longs to be experienced by us.

He wants us to be kingdom people with kingdom minds set on fulfilling His kingdom's purposes. He wants us to pray, as Jesus did, "Not my will, but Thy will be done." Because His is the kingdom, the power, and the glory.

There is only one God, and we are not Him. As King and Creator, God calls the shots. It is only when we align ourselves underneath His comprehensive hand that we will access His full power and authority in all spheres of life: personal, familial, church, and community.

As we learn how to govern ourselves under God, we then transform the institutions of family, church, and society from a biblically based kingdom worldview.

Under Him, we touch heaven and change earth.

To achieve our goal, we use a variety of strategies, approaches, and resources for reaching and equipping as many people as possible.

BROADCAST MEDIA

Millions of individuals experience *The Alternative with Dr. Tony Evans* through the daily radio broadcast playing on nearly **1,200 radio outlets** and in over **130 countries**. The broadcast can also be seen on several television networks and is viewable online at TonyEvans.org. You can also listen or view the daily broadcast by downloading the Tony Evans app for free in the App store. Over 4,000,000 message downloads occur each year.

LEADERSHIP TRAINING

The Tony Evans Training Center (TETC) facilitates educational programming that embodies the ministry philosophy of Dr. Tony Evans as expressed through the kingdom agenda. The training courses focus on leadership development and discipleship in the following five tracks:

- Bible & Theology
- Personal Growth
- Family and Relationships
- Church Health and Leadership Development
- Society and Community Impact Strategies

The TETC program includes courses for both local and online students. Furthermore, TETC programming includes course work for non-student attendees. Pastors, Christian leaders, and Christian laity, both local and at a distance, can seek out The Kingdom Agenda Certificate for personal, spiritual, and professional development. Some courses are valued for CEU credit as well as viable in transferring for college credit with our partner school(s).

The Kingdom Agenda Pastors (KAP) provides a *viable network* for *like-minded pastors* who embrace the Kingdom Agenda philosophy. Pastors have the opportunity to go deeper with

Dr. Tony Evans as they are given greater biblical knowledge, practical applications, and resources to impact individuals, families, churches, and communities. KAP welcomes *senior and associate pastors* of all churches. KAP also offers an annual Summit held each year in Dallas with intensive seminars, workshops, and resources.

Pastors' Wives Ministry, founded by Dr. Lois Evans, provides *counsel, encouragement,* and *spiritual resources* for pastors' wives as they serve with their husbands in the ministry. A primary focus of the ministry is the KAP Summit that offers senior pastors' wives a safe place to *reflect, renew,* and *relax* along with training in personal development, spiritual growth, and care for their emotional and physical well-being.

COMMUNITY IMPACT

National Church Adopt-A-School Initiative (NCAASI) prepares churches across the country to impact communities by using *public schools as the primary vehicle for effecting positive social change* in urban youth and families. Leaders of churches, school districts, faith-based organizations, and other nonprofit organizations are equipped with the knowledge and tools to *forge partnerships* and build *strong social service delivery systems.* This training is based on the comprehensive church-based community impact strategy conducted by Oak Cliff Bible Fellowship. It addresses such areas as economic development, education, housing, health revitalization, family renewal, and racial reconciliation. We assist churches in tailoring the model to meet specific needs of their communities while simultaneously addressing the spiritual and moral frame of reference. Training events are held annually in the Dallas area at Oak Cliff Bible Fellowship.

Athlete's Impact (AI) exists as an outreach both into and through the sports arena. Coaches are the most influential factor in young people's lives, even ahead of their parents. With the growing rise of fatherlessness in our culture, more young people are looking to their coaches for guidance, character development, practical needs, and hope. After coaches, athletes are next on the influencer scale. Athletes (whether professional or amateur) influence younger athletes and kids within their spheres of impact. Knowing this, we have made it our aim to equip and train coaches and athletes on how to live out and utilize their God-given roles for the benefit of the kingdom. We aim to do this through our iCoach App, weCoach Football Conference, as well as resources such as *The Playbook: A Life Strategy Guide for Athletes.*

RESOURCE DEVELOPMENT

We are fostering lifelong learning partnerships with the people we serve by providing a variety of published materials. Dr. Evans has published more than 100 unique titles based on over 40 years of preaching, whether that is in booklet, book, or Bible study format. The goal is to strengthen individuals in their walk with God and service to others.

For more information and a complimentary copy of
Dr. Evans' devotional newsletter, call (800) 800-3222
or write TUA at P.O. Box 4000, Dallas TX 75208,
or visit us online at www.TonyEvans.org

ACKNOWLEDGMENTS

———————— ♦ ————————

I am extremely grateful to the Moody Publishers family for their partnership with me in the development of this series of books for pastors and ministry leaders. Special thanks go to Greg Thornton who has been with me on this publishing journey with Moody Publishers from the start. I also want to thank Heather Hair for her collaboration on this manuscript. I want to acknowledge the Tony Evans Training Center, under the leadership of John Fortner, for the use of some course material which appears in this book. No book comes to life without editorial assistance, and so my thanks also includes Kevin Emmert, Michelle Sincock, and Duane Sherman.

Life is busy,

but Bible study is still possible.

tonyevanstraining.org

Explore the kingdom. Anytime, anywhere.

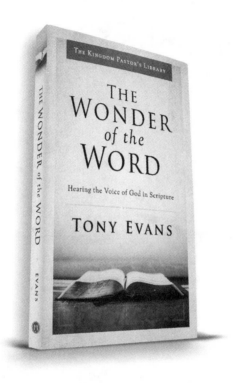

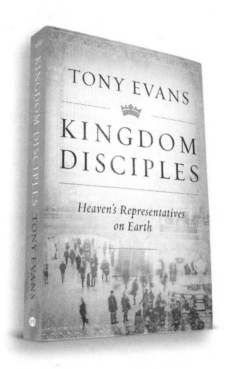

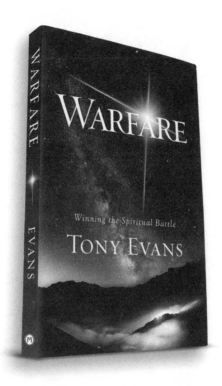